Integrity
in the
Workplace

Integrity
in the
Workplace

Blueprint for Today's Business Success

Steve Marr

Bridge-Logos
Orlando, Florida 32822

Bridge-Logos

Orlando, FL 32822 USA

Integrity in the Workplace
by Steve Marr

Library of Congress Catalog Card Number: 2006940656

International Standard Book Number 978-088270-339-8

G163.316.N.m701.35250

Contents

CHAPTER 1

What Is Integrity?

The Bible clearly tells us that we are to be people of integrity. Yet what is integrity? Jesus taught his disciples, "The ancients were told, 'You shall not make false vows, but shall fulfill your vows to the Lord.' But I say to you, make no oath at all ... let your statement be, 'Yes, yes' or 'No, no'" (Matthew 5:33-34, 37). Most people would agree that a morally respectable person keeps promises, doesn't lie, and doesn't cheat other people—but is there more to integrity than that? Are we people of integrity if we simply operate within the bounds of the law?

Burt and Peter Walbro were looking to retire. After being in business together for nearly thirty-five years, they wanted to sell their successful stamping company and pursue other interests. Many of their thirty employees had been loyal to them for more than ten years, and the brothers wanted to find a buyer who would be interested in continuing the business.

Max, a retired manufacturing CEO, offered to buy the business. He told the Walbro brothers that he wanted to manage the business himself and focus his skills and energy on growing the company. His background in manufacturing appeared be a major asset. He knew the business, as well as many of the company's vendors and customers. Max did his due diligence, examining the company's assets, customer list, equipment, and financial data. He checked out everything.

After a brief negotiation, a cash sales price of $2.5 million was agreed upon, and Max and the Walbros closed the deal. But the ink had no sooner dried on the contract before Max began to sell the company's assets and close the business. He sold the building for $1 million, and the machinery for $2.2 million. Not only that, but he was able to liquidate the overfunded pension plan and pocket $275,000. He also sold the accounts receivable list and other assets. In all, he netted $625,000 after liquidation expenses.

Was Max just a good, shrewd businessman? Were the Walbro brothers simply naïve and ripe for the picking? Max did nothing illegal, because the purchase contract did not specify that the business must be kept in operation. Even though the Walbros had made their desires clear, the promises were oral, and thus not enforceable. So, from a certain perspective, Max was honoring the letter of the law and did nothing wrong. He was merely a smart and savvy businessman who deserved to make a profit on his investment. But was he a person of integrity?

The prophet Hosea writes, "They spout empty words and make promises they don't intend to keep" (Hosea 10:4, NLT). Clearly, Max never intended to honor his commitment to continue the business; he just wanted to make a fast buck. The Walbro brothers knew they could have received more for the business by liquidating it, but they wanted to keep their loyal employees on the payroll. So, even though Max did nothing illegal, he essentially stole from the Walbro brothers and their staff.

Larry, a sales manager at a midsize company, was interviewing candidates for a new sales position. After interviewing eleven applicants, he narrowed his choices down to two finalists. He was in the process of checking references when he received a call from a close, longtime friend, who had steered business to Larry in the past, asking if his son Mark could be considered. Larry interviewed Mark and hired him on the spot. Was this fair to the others who had interviewed for the job? Larry didn't violate any nondiscrimination laws, and he didn't lie to anyone, because he hadn't promised the job to any of the candidates. But was the hiring process conducted with integrity?

Scripture tells us, "Be very careful what you do, for the Lord our God will have no part in unrighteousness, or partiality, or the taking of a bribe" (2 Chronicles 19:7). King Solomon writes, "To show partiality is not good" (Proverbs 28:21). Larry didn't break the law, or his word, but he did alter his normal hiring process, including not checking work-related references. He also permitted the past business referrals to cloud his judgment, in effect, allowing those referrals to become a bribe.

Mary was hired by Dr. Steve to work as a receptionist and records clerk. During her six months on the job, she had been five or ten minutes late to work two or three times every week. Dr. Steve had indirectly addressed the problem by saying "good afternoon" a few times when Mary walked in late, but he had never clearly communicated to her that the late arrivals were not acceptable, and that she needed to arrange to be at work consistently on time. Other than her chronic late arrivals, Mary's work was excellent.

One day, Mary walked in ten minutes late and Dr. Steve exploded. "You're fired," he said. "I'm sick and tired of your being late all the time. This is your last day." Dr. Steve had every right to let Mary go. He had never lied to her, and state law allowed for "employment at will." But did Dr. Steve use integrity in dealing with Mary?

Dr. Steve had never confronted Mary about her lateness, and he had never explained to her the consequences that would apply if she didn't change her behavior. When King David sinned by committing adultery and murder, the prophet Nathan confronted him with his sin. David then repented, and changed his behavior. When we sin against God, He gives us many opportunities to repent and change our behavior.

Appropriately confronting employees about performance issues and endeavoring to help them on a road to repentance and improved workplace behavior are key elements of business integrity.

Jim managed a City Auto Parts store for many years, bringing steady growth and an increase in profits for the owners. Over the years, the demographic makeup of the neighborhood began to change as many Spanish-speaking residents moved in, but Jim maintained an English-only policy with his salespeople. Several staff members and customers suggested that Jim should hire one or more bilingual employees to help with these customers and perhaps increase sales, but Jim took no action. Even as an increasing number of Spanish-speaking customers struggled to communicate their needs, and at times left without buying any merchandise, Jim was unwilling to change his policy. "If they're going to come to the U.S.," he insisted, "they need to learn to speak English." When several counter clerks tried to use their limited Spanish, Jim insisted that the store would use English only.

Over time, sales leveled off and then began to decline. Six months later, a new auto parts store opened up four blocks away. The new store carried fewer parts in stock and needed to order many parts for delivery in 24 to 48 hours, but their signs were in both English and Spanish, and most of their staff members were bilingual. Within two months, City Auto's sales had declined by 40 percent, and the owners decided to close the store, writing off a loss of $300,000 in closing costs, and putting twelve employees out of work. Jim went looking for a new job, believing he was the victim of circumstances and that there was nothing he could have done to keep the store going. He believed he had managed with integrity.

Jesus said, "Take care what you listen to. By your standard of measure it will be measured to you" (Mark 4:24). Job said, "If one ventures a word with you, will you become inpatient?" (Job 4:2). Solomon's son King Rehoboam "did not listen to the people" (1 Kings 12:15), and as a result the kingdom was divided. The Lord will often use other people to speak the truth to us, and we ignore their counsel at our peril. Effective leaders exercise sound judgment, often going against the grain. Business leaders don't need to put every issue to a staff vote, but they should develop the habit of effective listening, and they should seek the insight and wisdom of their employees who work on the front lines with customers. Jim violated an important biblical principle by not listening to the counsel of others, and the result was the closing of the store and the loss of a dozen jobs, including his.

In the chapters that follow, we will explore a biblical model of integrity that goes well beyond just telling the truth. As we understand how the Bible addresses issues of business integrity, we will learn how to conduct ourselves wisely and become more successful.

After the Enron debacle, I was asked by a chamber of commerce to give a talk on business integrity—specifically, how local businesses could avoid becoming mini Enrons—but they asked me to "leave that Bible stuff out of your talk." I politely explained that I have found the Bible to be a reliable guidebook for business integrity. If businesspeople don't adhere to biblical principles, they end up doing what is right in their own eyes (see Judges 21:25). The chamber instead invited an ethics professor from the university to speak. He defined ethics as not intending to harm anyone. Unfortunately, that standard isn't high enough. Executives at both Enron and World Com insisted they had not intended to harm anyone. Working with integrity requires that we establish a worthy basis for defining integrity and hold to that reliable standard.

If we have promised to complete a construction job for $75,000 and then discover that the cost of materials has increased, do we have the right to ask our customer to "be fair" and allow us to adjust the price? We have a responsibility to be diligent in our work. If we quote $75,000 for a job, we need to honor that price. If we focus on what seems fair to us, we will miss the greater mark, which is that God expects us to examine His word for guidance in every aspect of life and obediently apply that guidance.

"This book of the law shall not depart from your mouth, but you shall meditate on it day and night, so that you may be careful to do according to all that is written in it; for then you will make your way prosperous, and then you will have success" (Joshua 1:8). Following God's plan starts when we study the Scriptures and meditate on them to achieve understanding. Once we have studied God's Word, if we want to be successful, we must obediently apply His guidance. God doesn't promise to make us millionaires, or to meet our every whim, but He does promise us an abundant, successful life when we are obedient to Him.

Management gurus of every stripe have written thousands of books on how to succeed in business. Some of these books are very much on target, and others miss the mark. Management fads come and go; writers and speakers become popular and fall out of fashion; but the principles contained in the Bible are timeless and will never become ineffective. They will work for you whether you are CEO of a Fortune 500 company, a department manager, or the owner of a small business. Whether you are at the top, or want to get to the top, following biblical principles for success will pave your way.

When we see others who seem to flourish and make money regardless of their integrity, we may be tempted to join the party, to do "whatever it takes" to get ahead. However, Solomon offers wise counsel: "My son, if sinners entice you, do not give in to them" (Proverbs 1:10, NIV). Enron and WorldCom were once at the top of the charts, two apparently very successful companies. But several key players were not doing business with integrity—they had allowed themselves to be enticed by the siren song of success—and many of those folks are now in jail.

When Job fell on hard times, his friends attacked him verbally, saying, "But look, God will not reject a person of integrity, nor will he lend a hand to the wicked" (Job 8:20,

NLT). Though Job looked guilty to his accusers, he was declared innocent by God. Sin will always have consequences, even if they are not immediately or readily apparent. Scripture is very clear when it says that obedience and righteousness will ultimately bring blessings, while sin and disobedience will always bring judgment.

Moses wrote, "If you walk in my statutes and keep My commandments so as to carry them out, then I shall give you rains in their season, so that the land will yield its produce..." (Leviticus 26:3-4). However, the Scripture then sternly warns us, "but if you do not obey me..." and goes on for 24 verses explaining the penalties that will come as a direct result of disobedience.

Furthermore, the consequences of sin and lack of integrity will be far reaching. When King David took a census of Israel, despite the advice of his army commander and the will of God, 70,000 innocent Israelites died from a plague sent by the Lord (see 1 Chronicles 21:1-15). Likewise, many innocent employees, shareholders, and suppliers have paid a price for corporate malfeasance. Our integrity will touch those around us with blessings, but dishonesty will take others down with us.

CHAPTER 2

Delighting Your Customers

When Roman troops occupied Israel during the first century, a Hebrew citizen could be compelled to carry a soldier's supplies for one mile, and then he was free to go. Imagine how stunned a soldier would be if someone cheerfully offered to carry his supplies a second mile—in essence, delivering double the required service. Yet that's precisely what Jesus tells us we ought to do: "If someone forces you to go one mile, go with him two miles" (Matthew 5:41, NIV).

When dealing with customers, most businesspeople would agree that integrity means consistently delivering what we promise. But if we go beyond just doing what's expected, if we develop an attitude of not just doing the minimum, but *delighting* the customer by going the extra mile, it will set our businesses apart and bring in more customers in the future.

Who Is Your Customer?

If we don't understand who our customers are, we can't serve them effectively and our business will suffer. It may seem like a silly question to ask "who is our customer?" but often we have more than one customer to satisfy at a time, and our business success depends on understanding each one of those customers.

9

First, we have direct customers: the ones who pay our bills. We owe these customers our first and foremost loyalty. Next, we often have indirect customers, who are also very important to us. Indirect customers don't directly pay our bills, but they influence or control whether we get the business. For example, a motorist may have a car accident with the other driver at fault. The car owner would select a repair shop, obtain an estimate, and with the concurrence of the other driver's insurance company have the car repaired. The insurance company is the repair shop's direct customer, because they pay the bill, but the car owner is an equally importantly customer, because he or she decides which repair shop will get the business. The car owner may also direct others to use the repair shop's services, whereas the insurance company is unlikely to send much additional business to the repair shop, regardless of how pleased the insurance company is with the price and service.

Another example of an indirect customer is when a doctor refers a patient to a physical therapist. Often a doctor will recommend a therapist based on past experience. The direct charges for the therapy will be paid by the patient or an insurance company, but the doctor is an indirect customer. I know a physical therapist who thanks doctors for each referral and (with the appropriate client release) makes sure to send a report back to the referring physicians to help them complete their files. This therapist has generated additional business by wisely going the extra mile and providing a higher level of service to her indirect customers, the referring physicians.

At times we will have multiple customers for the same transaction. Often, prescription medicines are covered by insurance, either totally or, more commonly, with a co-payment. The attending pharmacist must satisfy both customers—the walk-in customer, who will insist on prompt, accurate service, pleasant surroundings and an agreeable pharmacy staff; and the insurance company, which will insist on competitive pricing and adherence to bookkeeping requirements. Failure to serve both customers well will result in lost business.

In addition to our outside customers, in every business we also have internal customers—people we serve within the organization. Smart businesspeople treat their internal customers with the same passion as they do their outside customers, because they understand that their business will only be effective when every customer is satisfied.

Isaiah writes, "So the craftsman encourages the smelter, and he who smoothes metal with the hammer encourages him who beats the anvil, saying of the soldering, 'It is good'; and he fastens it with nails" (Isaiah 41:7). The prophet gives us relevant insight into the importance of serving internal customers.

When the smelter does a poor job, impurities are left in the metal, which makes it impossible for the others in the craftsman's shop to produce a good finished job. Likewise, the anvil was used to rough out the material, and the better the rough work, the less hammer work would be needed. In other words, as each person in the process performs his or her tasks well, the work becomes more efficient and less costly. By serving their internal customers well, the metal smiths made it possible for the business to better serve its external customers. When we recognize *all* of our customers—internal and external, direct and indirect—and go the extra mile in serving them, the result will be an improved, more effective business.

Customer Empathy—Understanding and Meeting the Needs of Your Customers

Understanding our customers' needs and desires requires a lot of thought and effort. King Solomon writes, "The purposes of a man's heart are deep waters, but a man of understanding draws them out" (Proverbs 20:5, NIV). We cannot begin to offer solutions for customers until we understand their needs.

Businesses typically take one of two paths. Either they create a product or service and hope that customers will flock to buy

11

it, or they figure out what customers want or need and find a way to provide it. Quicken developed an excellent software package to assist people over the age of fifty to financially plan for retirement. The product worked well and fit a perceived need in the marketplace, but customers didn't buy it. Quicken lost sight of what their customers really wanted, and they lost millions of dollars as a result.

Starbucks, on the other hand, has mastered the art of understanding what their customers truly want and responding to those desires. That's why they've been able to build a retail empire selling a basic commodity—coffee. Through their advanced market research, Starbucks understood that a large, potential customer base was shopping for an experience, rather than just a cup of coffee. Anyone who wanted a plain cup of coffee could stop by a gas station, grab a quick cup, and move on. Instead, Starbucks developed premium brands, for which customers will pay two or three times the price of a regular cup of joe. In addition, the Starbucks experience includes comfortable, stylish places to sit, read, talk, or work. They created the atmosphere of a friendly meeting place. When I travel, I will occasionally hang out at Starbucks for an hour or two, checking my e-mail and working on my laptop. If you've ever been to a Starbucks, you know I'm not alone.

Our first job as business owners and managers is to develop the skill and habit of listening to our customers. King Solomon advises, "He who gives an answer before he hears, it is folly and shame to him" (Proverbs 18:13). We cannot offer solutions until we understand what the customer needs.

Some patrons are easier to connect with than others, but the key is to develop the best possible connection. An Oriental rug dealer greets people as they enter his store. He asks, "What room do you want to place a rug in?" The prospect may say that he or she is "just looking," with no specific rug or room in mind, but others will have specific ideas in mind. With these customers, the dealer follows up with questions regarding their budget, the size of the room, color schemes, furniture, and décor. Then he directs the shoppers directly to rugs that fit their needs. He has already effectively sifted through his products to zero in on what the customers want and need.

Customers give us both verbal and nonverbal signals, and both are important. When talking with customers, watch their body language. The Oriental rug dealer watches carefully when he mentions that a rug costs, say, $4,000. The customer may say that price is not a problem. But if the dealer sees the person stiffen, look surprised, or react in any negative way, he can sense that price is an issue—even if it goes unsaid—and begins to steer the prospect to lower priced merchandise.

When you ask a customer a question, *wait for the answer.* Silence, though uncomfortable at times, is a potent weapon in extracting effective information. Solomon advises, "[There is] a time to be silent and a time to speak" (Ecclesiastes 3:7, NIV). After you've asked a question, *listen*, and make sure the customer has finished responding before you speak again. Remember, as long as you're the one talking, you're not learning anything from your customer. Once you've heard and understood what your customers want, you can more efficiently and effectively meet their needs.

When a customer brings up a problem, or offers an objection, treat it as an opportunity to learn more, rather than become defensive. Customers who raise problems or objections are giving you an opportunity to strengthen your customer relationship. Communicating with customers is rather like peeling an onion; you take off one layer at a time. Though time consuming, it gets the job done.

Ask follow-up questions that engage your customers and provide you with needed information. Ask why the problem is a problem. What are the consequences to the customer if the situation is not improved? Why do they think that? How will it affect their lives or their business? Ask "how?" and "why?" questions repeatedly to dig deep into the customer's mind.

A word of caution is in order. Part of effective listening is determining how much a customer wants to become engaged in conversation. I have walked out of stores when salespeople have misjudged or ignored my level of interest. If they have approached me and I have politely explained that I just want to browse on my own and will let them know if I require assistance, and they continue to hover and close in every time I stop to look at something, I'll be out the door in no time. The key is to *listen* to your customers and *observe* their level of interest—and then respond accordingly.

Educate Your Customers

"In addition to being a wise man, the Preacher also taught the people knowledge" (Ecclesiastes 12:9). Customers may not understand what they want or need. Therefore, we need to provide effective instruction. Have you ever received a great product that you didn't completely understand? After we have listened well to our customers, we can begin the education process as needed.

Klondike Web Hosting Company received a call from a prospective customer who wanted to develop a Web site. Klondike's manager, Dan, asked what the customer wanted to accomplish with the site. Was it for informational purposes, to sell a product or service, or to create an interactive experience? If the site is for information only, Dan will ask what kind of information, facts, and image are to be communicated—and to whom. If the site is for sales, he asks what products or service will be marketed, and to whom.

Based on his experience and judgment, Dan then evaluates the feedback to determine whether the customer's goals can be achieved with a Web site. Understanding a customer's expectations is a key factor in delivering on those expectations. At times, Dan has to explain to his customers how merchandise can, and cannot, be effectively sold on the Internet. For example, Bill's Creative Designs, a fine jewelry maker, will not effectively sell work priced above $1,000 on the Internet unless

Bill has somehow established tremendous credibility in advance. Tiffany's, on the other hand, can sell expensive pieces online, because they already have a well-established reputation. Though Bill's integrity, value, and craftsmanship are first rate, it's very difficult to establish trust with customers over the Internet and to sell them expensive merchandise.

Other products may sell well online—witness the success of eBay and other auction sites, but just being on the Web doesn't guarantee sales. To be successful, a business will typically have to invest in substantial additional advertising to direct potential customers to the Web site. Dan has learned that he needs to take the time to instruct prospective customers about the realities of online marketing, and he will turn down work that he knows will not be successful. Though he occasionally passes up potentially lucrative opportunities, he has developed a list of truly happy clients, his business has grown steadily, and he has a waiting list of customers who want to enlist his services.

A health food store is another good example of a business that will need to educate its customers about the uses and benefits of various products. When time is invested in educating customers, they understand the benefits of doing business with your company and tend to become more loyal.

Offer Only Effective Solutions

Selling products and services that won't effectively meet a customer's needs just to get the sale is both unethical and counterproductive. When customers are disappointed, they don't come back. Worse, yet, they're likely to tell others about their disappointment. The prophet Jeremiah writes, "They offer superficial treatments for my people's mortal wound" (Jeremiah 6:14, NLT). When we offer poor, incomplete, or superficial solutions, we become guilty of a similar offense.

Remember the old movie *Miracle on Thirty-Fourth Street*? When the old man, Kris, took over the job of Santa Claus at Macy's department store, he sent customers to archrival

Gimbel's if Macy's didn't have what the customer wanted. Though Mr. Macy at first didn't think much of the idea, he later embraced it and instructed his employees to send customers elsewhere rather than push products on them that they didn't want. In the movie, customers marveled at the store's attitude, and as a result they shopped at Macy's even more. It works the same way in real life. When we determine to offer only effective solutions to our customers, we establish credibility and build trust.

I have purchased my business suits from the same store for thirty years. A few times, when I've tried on a suit and was going to purchase it, the salesman or alterations person would tell me that it just didn't look right, or that they couldn't alter that particular suit to fit me just right. The result was that even though they may have lost the sale for the moment, they gained a customer for life. Not only that, but whenever someone asks me where to buy a suit, I always refer them to my favorite store.

An important part of offering effective solutions is ensuring that problems are fixed and not just glossed over. If a health food store customer, for example, wants a comprehensive nutritional product but cannot afford the price, it would be unethical for the store employee to steer that customer to a substandard but less expensive product. It would be better for the employee to say that the store cannot offer a comprehensive product in the customer's price range, but that other products may give some, but not all, of the same benefits. The customer can then decide between spending more for the better product or settling for the lesser one. An unscrupulous employee would simply sell the lesser product as equal to the better one without explaining the difference in benefits.

Develop the Knowledge to Apply to
Your Customers' Needs

The prophet Hosea writes, "People without understanding are ruined" (Hosea 4:14). Likewise, businesspeople who don't understand their customers will eventually come to ruin. The first question we should ask ourselves is, "Who is—or who should be—my customer?" We may want to believe that everyone is a potential customer, but integrity demands that we determine the prospects we can most effectively serve.

The strength of any business is built on those things that they can do better than anyone else. Before we can focus on our customers, we must first understand our unique strengths. Only then can we effectively target the customers we can best serve.

Evergreen, a plant nursery, was struggling to compete with the large chain stores that were also selling yard plants. The small nursery had a higher cost structure than Wal-Mart and Lowe's, but they did offer fast delivery and planting services. Before they took the time to identify their core strengths, Evergreen was advertising to the mass market. However, those customers who wanted the lowest price were shopping at the "big box" stores rather than at Evergreen. Attempting to compete based on price alone was not only ineffective, it was also, I believe, unethical, because Evergreen was not the lowest-cost option.

When Evergreen took stock of their situation, they began advertising to customers who wanted larger trees and planting services. They worked at developing prospects who were in the market for these larger trees, a market they were best positioned to serve. As a result, they were able to operate with more integrity and their business began to flourish.

We need to ask ourselves, "What do my customers want and need, and do they know what they require?"

A CPA moved to a small town of 2,000 people, believing there was a market for his accounting and tax preparation services. He reasoned that because there were no other accountants in town, he could build a strong business because his potential clients would not want to drive to another town if he could offer the service locally.

However, after he set up shop, he learned that the 2,000 people in town represented only 650 households, and only 175 of those used any tax service at all. Moreover, only thirty-five households had tax returns that were complex enough to require a CPA—too few to support an accounting practice. Worse yet, most of the thirty-five households that needed a CPA already had an established relationship with one, and they wouldn't change just because a new CPA moved into town. If the CPA had conducted an in-depth review of the market before he made the move, he probably wouldn't have relocated.

Pete, a telephone system salesman, was asked to propose a new system for a company in his territory. He was told that the total budget was $10,000. After reviewing the customer's specifications, Pete realized that it would cost $13,000 for a system that would meet 100 percent of the company's needs. He could put together a system for $8,900 that would meet most of the customer's requirements, but it would not be the complete package the customer wanted. He presented both options and explained the differences. The customer could either pay a few thousand dollars more to get exactly what they wanted, or they could lower their expectations and get a system that fit their budget. In the end, Pete lost the bid to Sam, a competitor who sold a similar system to Pete's $8,900 option. The difference was that Sam promised the company that the budget system would do everything they wanted. Eighteen months later, when Sam's system failed to meet expectations, the company awarded Pete a new contract for a $17,000 system. He subsequently sold more than $100,000 in new equipment to the growing company because of the trust he had built by working with integrity right from the start.

Proactively Address Customer Service Needs

Most businesspeople believe in providing customer service. However, they often wait until a customer complains or a problem becomes obvious before they take action. A wise business leader, on the other hand, steps in early, when problems are small and manageable.

King Rehoboam, Solomon's son, was advised to lighten the tax load on the people of Israel. His advisors told him, "If you will be a servant to these people today, and serve them, and answer them, and speak good words to them, then they will be your servants forever" (1 Kings 12:7, NKJV). But when Rehoboam failed to respond to the people, the kingdom was torn in two and never recovered.

Dan's Family Restaurant was well located and enjoyed a good flow of business. The quality of food and service was inconsistent, and customers sometimes complained, but most customers came back because the problems weren't that bad and the location was convenient. Dan took some steps to improve the restaurant, but he never fully committed to fixing the problems. Within the next year, however, three new restaurants opened up nearby, and two of them provided better quality, service, and value. Presented with several choices now, customers began to flock to Dan's competitors, and two years later he was out of business. If Dan had responded proactively, before competition forced him to respond, he would have locked up a solid and loyal clientele.

Radcliff Manufacturing made electronic control parts for industrial cooking ovens. When a vital overseas supplier began running behind on delivery of some needed parts, Radcliff's manufacturing manager immediately contacted them to find out which parts could be shipped, and by when.

At the same time, Radcliff's sales department began notifying customers to explain the delays. For customers who could wait longer for delivery, Radcliff adjusted their schedules; but for customers who would otherwise be adversely affected by the delays, Radcliff shipped parts by air freight, at a higher expense. By being proactive, Radcliff allowed their customers to adjust to the situation before they were hurt by it.

I once held a job as a purchasing agent and bought copy paper in lots of fifteen to twenty boxes at a time. The salesman told me that if I could order a full pallet of forty boxes, the paper could be shipped directly from the supplier at a significant cost savings. The salesman could have continued to sell me the smaller lots at a higher margin, but he earned my trust and cemented our relationship by being proactive and working with integrity.

A key step in the process of addressing customer service needs is the establishment of product-quality and service-level benchmarks. Once these standards are in place, we must take care to ensure that we continually meet them. When we see that a product or delivery has fallen short, we must take quick action, *before* our customers complain. Of course, an absence of complaints does not mean an absence of lost customers, or customers at risk. An airline I fly regularly may think I am a loyal customer because of my regular travel. But I am not. My airline decisions are based on schedule and price, not on my satisfaction with a particular carrier.

A second important piece of the customer service puzzle is the innovation of new ideas. By staying on the cutting edge, we develop timely solutions for our customers before they can depart for better options. Back in the days when computer technology was first being introduced to the printing industry, Larry at Desert Pacific Printing began using computers in his prepress department. In those days, it was not possible to create a plate directly from a computer image, but they could print out the image and burn the plate photographically, the same way they always had. Larry started fiddling with developing a system for printing directly from the computer data, and he started gaining new customers as a result. Today, almost all printing is done from computers, but the first to understand the paradigm shift were able to gain a business advantage over their competitors.

Finally, we need to instill the habit of settling issues with customers promptly. Jesus said, "Make friends quickly with your opponent at law while you are with him on the way" (Matthew 5:25). Granting a refund, credit, or replacement will generate little customer goodwill if they feel as if they are pulling teeth to get satisfaction. Wal-Mart has a liberal return policy, and as a result they have strengthened their customer relationships.

When a customer raises a concern, consider the following questions:
- Is the customer right?
- Have we made a mistake?
- What could we have done better?
- Has the customer taken on the burden of our mistake?
- What can we do to make the situation right?

Whatever you do, avoid being defensive. If you made a mistake and need to absorb some cost or expend extra effort to make the situation right, do it promptly. When a bank made a $300 error in my account, I had to make four personal visits to the branch and eight phone calls to resolve the problem. I finally received the credit I was due, but at that point any goodwill was long gone.

When Saul was king of Israel, he had murdered a large number of Gibeonites in violation of a long-standing treaty. When David succeeded Saul on the throne, he understood that he needed to rectify the situation with the Gibeonites. He met with their leaders, and asked, "What can I do for you to make amends?" (2 Samuel 21:3, NLT). Notice that David didn't pass off responsibility to Saul. Instead, he accepted responsibility to make the situation right. Likewise, when our company falls short, we must take responsibility for our company and our colleagues and make the situation right.

Commit Your Company to
Quality in Products and Services

Quality is important to every business. The Lord set the standard when He created the world: "And God saw all that He had made, and behold, it was very good" (Genesis 1:31, NASB). The apostle Paul writes, "Each man's work will become evident; for the day will show it" (1 Corinthians 3:13, NASB).

We need to keep in mind that quality standards will vary, depending on the product or service in question. For example, a newspaper will have a different standard than a fashion magazine for print quality, simply based on the type of paper and the printing processes they use. But even though the two publications will look and feel different, both should have high-quality design, layout, editing, and content. Using newsprint instead of glossy paper stock is not unethical for a newspaper, but putting out a poorly written paper would be.

We need to establish standards for our businesses based on our corporate mission and vision statements, and the commitments made to customers. Moses writes, "See that you make them after the pattern for them, which was shown to you on the mountain" (Exodus 25:40). God (and Moses) understood that the people needed to be given a pattern by which to establish a standard of excellence.

To do this, we first need to define specifically what level of service and quality will be acceptable to you and your customers. Sam's Club, for example, does not provide bags to its customers, as a way of keeping costs low. Most supermarkets offer simple plastic or paper bags; and an upscale department store like Saks Fifth Avenue supplies a magnificent shopping bag with each purchase.

UPS and FedEx provide different levels of service, depending on what the customer wants and is willing to pay for. It's not unethical to offer next-day service for $40 while charging $12 to deliver the same package by ground in one week. The ethical problem arises when we fail to deliver the quality or level of service that was promised to the customer.

Establishing standards is a good first step, but we must document those standards and communicate them clearly to our employees to ensure consistent performance. Midwest Medical Supply mailed 150 invoices each day and had five percent returned because of billing errors. The accounts receivable department established a standard that 99.5 percent of invoices must be correct. Management established a price file for each customer, making correct pricing easier, and established a policy that price changes were to be updated daily for each customer, thereby further eliminating errors. Staff were trained to utilize the new system and their accuracy rate soon met the 99.5 percent goal. Midwest Medical could have let the problem slide, believing that their customers were not really harmed by having to send bills back for correction. But management realized that billing accuracy was an issue of integrity and credibility, and that billing errors undermined their customers' faith in Midwest Medical.

Monitor Your Standards

Establishing the right standards is the first step, but those standards must be monitored to ensure continual compliance. King Solomon writes, "He who tends the fig tree will eat its fruit" (Proverbs 27:18). A fig tree, like any fruit tree, needs to be tended to regularly to look for signs of disease, lack of water, insect infestation, or leaf wilt. Likewise, we need to monitor our business standards every day to ensure that we are consistently maintaining our standards. Just saying that we give good service doesn't make it so.

Some businesses are easier to monitor than others, but standards can be tracked in every operation. Manufacturing companies can calculate the number of items that fail to meet standards, a copy servicing company can ensure that callbacks are limited, and restaurants can monitor the number of customer complaints received. When issues arise, correct them systematically, rather than just slapping on a Band-Aid. Customers hate to experience the same problem twice, and our costs increase when we keep scrambling to respond to individual customer issues. Take the time to follow up with customers to make sure that they are satisfied, the adjustment was satisfactory, and the improvement has lasted.

23

Fair Treatment and Pricing

"You shall not have in your bag differing weights, a large and a small. You shall not have in your house differing measures, a large and a small" (Deuteronomy 25:13-14). Here, Moses is referring to the practice of unscrupulous merchants who would cheat people by using two sets of weights. Customers who were poor would rarely have their own set of weights, so the merchant's scales would have to be used. A "pound" weight that was actually only fourteen or fifteen ounces would cheat the customer and pad the merchant's profits. Vendors knew that their wealthier customers might have their own set of weights, and thus the sellers would use their honest set of weights to avoid being caught cheating.

Based on the principle of standard weights—giving every customer the benefit of a fair deal—price discrimination is wrong, unless there is good justification. The world may say *caveat emptor*, "let the buyer beware," but taking advantage of a person's lack of knowledge or negotiating skills is wrong.

An electric utility that charges lower rates for off-hour use is an example of fair pricing, because the lower price is available to everyone. Volume discounts also are fine, because a customer who buys 300 boxes of paper is entitled to a lower price than someone who only buys two boxes. Some customers have a lower sales cost, and thus the savings can be passed along to them in the form of a discount, and some customers will sign long-term contracts to get a better price. These situations are ethically acceptable, because the customer is in a sense earning the discount. Supply and demand is also a factor. Hotels charge more in high tourist season, when demand is high, and less in the off season, to attract customers. An Arizona window washing company offers summer discounts because business is slower during the summer when many seasonal residents are gone.

Ezekiel writes, "Let not the buyer rejoice nor the seller mourn" (Ezekiel 7:12), suggesting a balance in pricing. At times, we may have tremendous pricing power that can be used to extract large profits. Though I am a strong free-market advocate, I caution businesses against using their pricing power indiscriminately. Market forces will sometimes cause large increases in costs, such as we've seen with gasoline, paper, and plastics. Most businesses can't control these increases, but taking unreasonable advantage of the market can lead to our long-term downfall. Customers may pay our high prices because there is no alternative, but at the cost of our long-term relationships. At the first opportunity, those customers may pay us back by changing suppliers.

Wise business leaders seek to provide a stable, consistent level of service rather than furnish different levels of service based on customer demands. Offering different levels of service for the same price is discrimination. That is not to say we shouldn't respond to urgent requests, but our policies should be even-handed. If we put customers equally on the rush-order list, when requested, that's great. However, if we pace one order ahead of another simply because the customer is demanding, then discrimination has occurred.

Case Study: Customer Service

Great American Furniture owns seventeen furniture companies that manufacture and sell all types of furniture to stores throughout the United States. The company developed a standard practice that all orders will be shipped within 25 working days.

Kankakee Furniture Company of Illinois, a subsidiary of Great American, developed its own system of entering orders and confirming expected shipping dates with customers. Orders are tracked, performance records are kept, and a report is generated confirming that shipments are shipped within the agreed-upon dates.

When Kankakee Furniture began experiencing production problems—everything from manufacturing equipment breakdowns to a shortage of trained personnel—their ability to meet their expected delivery schedule began to slip. Business was still good, but the company's performance was below standard. When orders were placed, customers were told that deliveries would be made within 30 to 40 days, instead of the usual 25. Some customers agreed to this schedule, but others decided to cancel their orders. When a customer accepted a later delivery date, the agreed-upon shipping date was entered into the computer. But if a customer threatened to cancel an order, the plant manager would adjust the production schedule, putting those pieces ahead of other work, in order to meet the 25-day standard and preserve the customer relationship.

In other cases when a customer threatened to cancel an order, the manager agreed to a special discount, canceling material-upgrade charges on some orders. The order was placed with the longer delivery time and the special discount.

A senior manager from Great American Furniture who was reviewing operations was appalled that the 25-day shipping standard was not being met. In response, the Kankakee plant manager replied, "I don't see why you're upset; we have a 98 percent success rate of shipping on or before the dates agreed upon with our customers."

Questions:
- Was the manager of Kankakee Furniture delivering furniture consistently on the promised dates?
- Was furniture being delivered consistently on the dates their customers wanted?
- What three biblical principles of integrity were violated, and how?

CHAPTER   3

Stewardship Responsibility

Stewardship is a key integrity issue, because God owns everything in the world and has given us responsibility for managing it. David writes, "Yours, O Lord, is the greatness and the power and the glory and the victory and the majesty, indeed everything that is in the heavens and the earth; Yours is the dominion, O Lord, and You exalt Yourself as head over all" (1 Chronicles 29:11). When we take care and use resources wisely and effectively, we are working increasingly for the Lord, not ourselves. But if we are unwise or lazy, we are literally squandering the Lord's resources.

Daniel had many enemies who wanted to bring him down for their own selfish gain, but "they could find no corruption in him, because he was trustworthy and neither corrupt nor negligent" (Daniel 6:4, NIV). How many of us would live up to Daniel's standard of integrity? Our businesses and assets are not for our own pleasure, but to glorify God. God expects far more from us than just getting by; He wants us to glorify Him in and through our businesses.

Effective Stewardship Over Time and Treasure
First, to be effective stewards over our time and treasure, we must understand what is happening with the resources

entrusted to us. King Solomon instructs, "Know well the condition of your flocks, and pay attention to your herds; for riches are not forever" (Proverbs 27:23-24). In Solomon's time, a person's flocks were an important measurement of wealth. A shepherd might look over a flock of two thousand sheep and feel wealthy. However, that wealth could be fleeting. Each day, the shepherd must check the flock. If some sheep turned up missing, the shepherd would have to find them before they wandered too far; if predatory animals were attacking the flock, the shepherd would have to arrange for additional security before more damage was done. At the first sign of illness, the affected sheep needed to be treated and quarantined to keep the disease from spreading. A herd that was not carefully watched could disappear in a few weeks, leaving the owner broke. The same diligence required in King Solomon's time is needed today in our businesses.

"Management by walking around" is a common phrase and a good management tool. A restaurant owner can learn a lot by watching how the food is served, and how customers respond. Manufacturing executives can learn a lot of valuable information by walking the factory floor, asking questions, and soliciting feedback. The questions they ask should include the following: What do you like most about working here? What do you like least? Is there any way your job could be made easier or more efficient? The goal is to establish open and honest communication at all levels of a company. When customers or employees give us feedback, even negative feedback, we need to listen carefully and not become defensive or we will cut off the very communication we need in order to be effective.

First Determine What Is Important

We are bombarded with nonstop demands, more demands than we can possibly meet in a day. In order to be effective stewards, we need to determine what is important and make sure those items get completed well.

Every business has critical success factors—items that if done well will ensure that the business will do well. In your own business, identify three to seven key factors that have a major effect on your company. Each success factor must be measurable, controllable, and high impact.

For example, an HVAC contractor was billing to customers only forty percent of the hours actually worked. Inefficient work assignments, failure to carry the right inventory on trucks for jobs, and poor execution contributed to the company's substandard performance. The owners identified billable time as a key critical success factor. Over time, they increased their efficiency factor from forty percent to sixty percent, generating a consistent gain in profits.

Every truck was checked in the morning to verify that all parts were on board for scheduled jobs, thus eliminating the need for additional parts runs. The dispatchers were trained to ask more qualifying questions to determine exactly what the customer needed and which parts to place on the truck.

An Internet-based sales organization budgeted 30 percent of their selling price toward marketing expenses. The company was able to advertise in a variety of ways, including banner ads, pay-per-clicks, and email campaigns. The key success factor was to measure each marketing tactic to make sure that their sales cost stayed at, or below, thirty percent.

A business similar to the Designed to Sell television company was able to close sales eighty percent of the time they were invited into a client's home to make a presentation. For this business, the critical success factor was the number of times they could get into the customer's living room.

Other businesses may identify the percentage of repeat customers as a key factor. Regardless of what business we're in, we cannot effectively watch our flocks until we have determined what is important for our business success. Then, we must measure those factors and see to it that we effectively execute those factors.

Follow Up Immediately
When You See a Potential Problem

Business owners, executives, and managers commonly believe that if they see no evil or hear no evil, then there is no evil. In reality, however, King Solomon's advice is clear: "Don't try to avoid responsibility by saying you didn't know about it" (Proverbs 24:12, NLT). We are responsible for what we know, and what we *should* know.

Moses gives us a clear word picture to demonstrate the increased responsibility that applies after we have been given a warning: "And if an ox gores a man or a woman to death, the ox shall surely be stoned…but the owner of the ox shall go unpunished. If, however, an ox was previously in the habit of goring and its owner has been warned, yet does not confine it, and it kills a man or a woman, the ox shall be stoned and its owner also shall be put to death" (Exodus 21:28-29). Once the owner had been warned, he or she was responsible for restraining the ox.

Most problems start small and escalate. Even at a company such as Enron, the first steps were technically legal but deceitful. If the leaders had stopped what they were doing early, no one would have gone to jail.

Next, they stepped over the line, but just barely. After a while, the malfeasance was so complete that no one knew the true condition of the company.

Most disasters give us advance warning. A restaurant will typically receive several warnings from the health department before failing an inspection outright and having its license suspended. In another case, a Kentucky fireworks plant received six safety violation notices before a fatal explosion killed several workers. The factory owners were indicted on charges of negligent homicide, based on their failure to remedy the past safety violations.

It is incumbent upon owners, managers, and supervisors to know the condition of their flocks. If an employee starts to ignore instructions, for example, and we forgo discipline because the issues are minor, we should be prepared for when the violations become more frequent and create serious problems for our business. Wise leaders will develop a regular habit of thoroughly investigating problems as they surface, to avoid additional harm from later affecting the business.

Proactively Maintain Property and Equipment

Part of good stewardship is keeping our property, tools, and equipment in good repair. "If a man is lazy, the rafters sag; if his hands are idle, the house leaks" (Ecclesiastes 10:18, NIV). Here, King Solomon illustrates that neglect over a very long period of time has devastating consequences. Many tasks can be deferred for a while, but if we don't complete them in a timely manner, we risk damaging our business and undermining our good stewardship.

First, we must take a realistic look at our properties. Buildings require regular maintenance and we should budget a reasonable amount of money for upkeep. If we neglect to repair the roof, it may spring a leak, creating a more expensive repair later. Moreover, the leak will also damage the ceiling, walls, and carpeting. By failing to do basic maintenance, we become poor stewards of our resources. If the budget is tight and we think we do not have the money to allocate to repairs, we should consider a value equation; namely, the value that will be lost if repairs are not completed.

One of my clients had a cash-flow shortage, and as a result was deferring all kinds of maintenance items, including resurfacing the parking lot. I pointed out that if the lot was not sealed soon, the small cracks would worsen and a much more expensive major repair would be needed. Allowing the deterioration to continue was poor stewardship, and bad business.

A key issue faced by many small business owners is not providing funds in the budget for repair and replacement of tools and equipment. These are very real costs, and if we cannot afford to place them in our budget, we need to take a hard look at our operation. A contractor, one of my clients, was losing money. After reviewing his finances, I could see that the big problem was tool expense—the replacement and repair of tools such as broken drill bits, a power motor that burned out, or unexpected truck repairs. I advised him to calculate and add to every job a cost factor that would include the average expense of tool replacement and repair. My client was concerned that he would start pricing himself out of the market if he raised prices even a little bit. I explained that he was slowly going broke by not accounting for all his actual expenses, and his choice was either to bid jobs based on his actual costs, including tool expense, or close up the business and work for another contractor.

Another aspect of maintaining our equipment is to stay current and competitive. Computers for example, may have a four-year actual life, but their competitive life is really only eighteen months. Depending on your business, you should start investing for the future equipment you'll need to get and stay on top. Yahoo and eBay once thought that if they could get to the top of the market, they could slow down their spending on technology. But the opposite turned out to be true; they continue to pour hundreds of millions of dollars into their businesses to keep their competitive edge.

The inability to budget for ongoing repairs, maintenance, and future upgrades is a stealth business killer. We need to make sure we are able to include these costs in our budgets, or the result will be that our business rafters will sag, and our roofs will leak.

Make Effective Use of Your Time

"Teach us to make the most of our time, so that we may grow in wisdom" (Psalm 90:12, NLT). Moses' prayer is just as relevant today for business leaders as it was when he first spoke the words. Pressures from customers, government agencies, competitors, and bosses put all of us under time pressure. As people of integrity, we need to make every day count on the job.

First, plan each day by creating a prioritized list of things to do, and then work that list. Ask yourself how each task will affect your customers and your business. Consider whether an undertaking will help you achieve or improve a critical success factor. Staying on task and focused is a challenge for us all.

We need to avoid wasting time. Keeping up with coworkers is okay, but we don't need to chat for twenty minutes about last night's game or the latest TV show. And though most of us will make or receive personal phone calls, we need to keep the number, and duration, to a minimum.

Internet usage is a big time waster. Online gambling and pornography may grab the headlines, but by some estimates more than $130 billion of work time is wasted each year by employees who use the Internet during business hours for nonbusiness reasons—whether it's making vacation reservations, perusing Web MD, buying and selling on eBay, or checking out gardening sites. When we are at work, we have a responsibility to stay on task. Surfing the Web is best suited for home, the library, or after work hours.

Work attendance is a key aspect of making the most of our time. From my perspective, sick days are only to be used when one is actually sick. Calling in sick in order to go to the beach or a ballgame, or to run errands or catch up on household chores is not ethical. Some companies have a personal leave policy that permits employees to take time off for various personal reasons—including illness and medical appointments. But if your company has only a sick day policy, you should reserve those days only for when you are sick.

Personal stewardship of our health is another key factor. We need to take reasonably good care of ourselves and get adequate rest. Some people will get sick more often than others, but we need to do what we can to eat right, exercise, and stay healthy.

I managed one person who was a diabetic, but who disregarded her doctor's instructions. Instead of watching what she ate, she snacked on high-sugar foods like jelly doughnuts.

She also failed to exercise and was lax about maintaining her blood-testing schedule. As a result, she took many sick days. I believe that she was genuinely sick on these days, but she could have made a more serious effort to comply with her doctor's instructions, which would have helped her manage her illness and achieve better health.

Another person I managed was a party person. He would stay out late at night carousing, and would frequently call in sick or come in late as a result. We're all susceptible to illness, and we can't always avoid accidents or surgeries, but part of working with integrity is doing everything we can to stay healthy and well-rested.

Case Study: Stewardship

Bob and Nancy owned a small grocery store that specialized in quality and selection of fresh fruits and vegetables. Customers enjoyed being able to purchase items not available elsewhere, and the quality was always top notch. After 35 years of running the store, the couple decided to reduce the amount of time they worked and allow their sons, Peter and Mark, to start taking over the business.

Mark took the responsibility of going to the farmer's market early in the morning to select the new produce, and he made several changes in purchasing. First, to obtain lower prices and boost profit margins, he bought some of the exotic items in larger quantities. As a result, these items remained on the shelf longer at the store, and some lost quality. Mark also started buying regular produce, but of a slightly lower quality, from different suppliers. The store's retail prices, however, remained the same. Peter was responsible for maintaining the store, and he also made several changes. He turned up the temperature slightly in the cooler to save money on electricity, and he stopped taking time each week to clean the refrigeration units. He also reduced staffing by one employee, which resulted in a cutback in cleaning—the floor was cleaned less often, the windows became dirty, and garbage started accumulating in the back storeroom. When restocking the produce shelves, Peter and Mark tended to accomplish the task quickly, at times bruising fruit or not presenting merchandise well.

At first, a few customers commented that the quality had slipped a bit, and sales fell slightly, but profits actually increased due to the lower cost of goods sold and savings on electricity. Bob and Nancy, who stopped by the store infrequently, questioned Mark and Peter about the slight drop in sales. The young men insisted that customers were happy, and proudly pointed to the increased profits.

A year later, sales had dropped by twenty percent, and the perennially profitable store was close to losing money. Several failures in the produce cooling system had resulted in several thousand dollars of lost product.

Questions:
- What should Bob and Nancy have done differently?
- As far as their customers were concerned, did Mark and Peter violate any biblical principles in pricing goods?
- What steps could Mark and Peter have taken to keep customers happy?
- What Biblical principles were violated in their operation of the business?

Doing What We Say We Will Do

M ost people would agree that keeping promises is a cornerstone of business integrity. Scripture is clear that we need to keep our word. For example, the prophet Jeremiah writes, "Go ahead and confirm your vows, and certainly perform your vows!" (Jeremiah 44:25).

Today, many businesses promise *too much*. As King Solomon advised, "It is better that you should not vow than that you should vow and not pay" (Ecclesiastes 5:5). Declining to make a promise is not a sin, but failing to honor a promise is.

Jesus taught, "Simply let your 'Yes' be 'Yes,' and your 'No,' 'No'" (Matthew 5:37, NIV). Simply put, a promise is any statement, oral or written, by which we say that we will do something. Telling a customer that we will call back today, or saying to a boss that we will have a report done today, is a promise. The consequences of failing to follow through on a promise may differ, but biblically there is no difference.

Jesus instructed us to count the cost before we make commitments (see Luke 14:28-32). So, before we give our word to someone, we must count the cost of following through and doing what we say we will do. In the spirit of letting our "Yes" be "Yes," and our "No," "No," we must also use clarifying words to differentiate between *trying* to do something and *promising* to do something. We shouldn't promise unless we've counted the cost and we're ready, willing, and able to deliver.

Most businesspeople don't intend to deceive when making quick promises, but Scripture does not differentiate between our intent and our performance. The Bible clearly teaches that we must keep our vows and promises. When we accept an order for delivery on Monday, we had better have a reasonable expectation that our promise is valid and will be kept.

Follow-through will always be necessary to keep our promises. We may need to write down our commitments, or leave ourselves a voice mail message, or devise another system that works. But the responsibility falls on the one making the promise, not on the recipient of the promise. In a perfect world, we would keep every promise, every time, and follow-up would never be necessary. However, we live in an imperfect, fallen world, where other factors come into play. Nevertheless, the responsibility is still ours to follow through on our promises.

Some people confuse their intention to do something with actually doing it. But if we fail to honor a promise, is a good excuse good enough? Does a promise not kept plus a great reason for not keeping our promise equal the same as keeping our word? I don't think so.

Promises to Customers

Every business transaction has two parts: the responsibility of the purchaser, and the responsibility of the seller. Generally, the buyer is responsible for being clear on what is wanted, and for paying for what is received. The seller is responsible to deliver everything exactly as promised.

Micah writes, "Can I justify wicked scales and a bag of deceptive weights?" (Micah 6:11). Anytime we deliver less than we have promised—in terms of quality, quantity, or service— we have in effect used a bag of deceptive weights. No one would disagree that a customer who orders and pays for fifty pounds of concrete, but receives only 48 pounds, is a victim of deceptive weights. But what about when a furniture store promises a delivery on Monday, but misses the delivery and tries to reschedule for Wednesday? Is that not also the same principle of deceptive weights? A buyer expects to receive both the item and the agreed-upon service.

An office equipment service company sold contracts agreeing to service their equipment for a set monthly fee. They also promised to respond within four hours when a service call was placed. Most calls were made in a timely fashion, but 25 percent of the time the service technician arrived late— sometimes as late as the next day. When a customer called to discuss the late arrivals, the service manager said, "We work hard, we try, we do the best we can, we respond fast, but sometimes our technicians are a long way away." Never once did he acknowledge that the four-hour service commitment was not being met. Though we occasionally may fall short, if we promise four-hour service and deliver less, then we have failed to deliver on our promise.

When we fail to deliver on a promise, we need to assume the consequences rather than transferring the burden to our customer. For example, if we promise to ship by UPS ground today, but forget to process the order, should we insist that the customer pay air freight to get their delivery on time? No. It's unreasonable and unethical to ask a customer to absorb an additional charge for something that is not their responsibility. The customer may be willing to accept a ground shipment made late, but we should never assume this is okay or expect the customer to pay the higher air freight cost if a delay in delivery is not acceptable. We must assume the responsibility of bearing the consequences of our shortfalls.

When we accept the consequences, we will quickly become far more disciplined and effective in our operations. When we ask the customer to pay the price, we have no motivation for improvement. I once drove 250 miles round-trip to accept a furniture delivery. When the delivery didn't arrive and I called to follow up, the dispatcher told me that the delivery had been rescheduled because of a shortage of drivers that day. I explained that I had driven 250 miles, used up my gas, wasted my time, and that I expected a price reduction of $50 to cover my expenses. The company's first response was that it wasn't their fault and the store didn't give credits. I explained that unless the credit was granted, I would cancel the order and insist on a full refund. The issue became a matter of principle to me, in part because two previous deliveries from the same store had also not been delivered on time. Because I hadn't asked for a credit the first two times (and presumably other customers had let the company off the hook as well), the store owners thought they could just shrug off the problem, ignore their promise, and pay no price for it. They apparently had no incentive to fix the problem.

Other customer promises are not part of a sales transaction, but they do constitute a vow. When we promise to call back today, to send out a price quote by the end of the week, or pack future orders in larger boxes, we have made a commitment that must be honored.

The bottom line is that we must count the cost of all promises and then deliver on what we have said. When we are not certain that we can deliver, we need to avoid making a promise. Perhaps we say that we will try to ship today, but with no guarantees; or we say we will send out the quote this week, if possible, but with the backlog we have it may not be until next Tuesday. (Of course, then we had better make sure to get the quote out by Tuesday.)

Promises to Employees

When we make promises to our employees, we must follow through just as we would with our best customers. King Solomon writes, "Hope deferred makes the heart sick" (Proverbs 13:12). When we make promises to our employees and then fail to honor those promises, we lose their trust and undermine their morale.

40

When staff members ask for time off, or for special assistance, or have a question about benefits and we promise to get back to them, we have made a vow that we must keep.

There are three primary reasons why we fail to follow through on promises to employees. First, we may believe the issue isn't very important, so we pass it off. However, the issue may be important to our staff. Second, we may just forget. That's why we need to develop a follow-up system that works for us. Finally, we may not want to deal with an issue, such as a request for a raise. We may know that a raise is not in order, but we don't want to have a confrontational discussion. However, stalling or failing to respond will only make the problem worse.

Promises to Vendors

When we are the purchasers, we have certain responsibilities. We need to be clear about what we expect, and we must agree to the price, delivery, and payment terms offered. We have a responsibility to pay our invoices within the agreed terms. Solomon writes, "Do not withhold good from those to whom it is due, when it is in your power to do it" (Proverbs 3:27). Late payments, for example, without justification, are wrong.

If issues arise that may delay our payments, we need to resolve them promptly. I know of a Christian-owned company that has 30-day payment terms with one of its vendors. Invoices are reviewed upon receipt and are set up to pay within thirty days. However, if an error is discovered, the invoice is returned within thirty days, with a request to re-bill, thus generating another thirty-day payment cycle. Though the customer was technically within their rights in complying with the payment terms, I believe that the practice lacked integrity. They should have notified their vendors as soon as a problem was discovered and done everything they could to comply with the original terms of sale. Certainly it was within their power to do it.

When negotiating volume discounts from the buyer's side, we need to be honest about our expected purchasing volume.

Granted, our needs may change, but we should provide our true forecast volume, rather than saying we will buy five hundred electric motors to get a better price when we know full well that our true volume will be closer to one hundred units. When we have a contract or other fixed agreement, we must stick with the agreed price. When business is slow, companies like General Motors have unilaterally demanded lower prices from their suppliers. Asking for help is one thing; demanding discounts on contract prices is something else.

Don't make your vendors pay unreasonably for mistakes. Thought it's reasonable and appropriate to hold suppliers accountable for their promises, don't make unnecessary demands just because someone makes a mistake. When an order is shipped late, for example, don't demand overnight air freight service, unless expedited delivery is important and necessary.

We should also treat our vendors with kindness and respect. Being in the driver's seat does not give us license to be rude, loud, or ill-mannered. Difficult situations can be negotiated even as we maintain our kind and reasonable demeanor.

Promises to Bosses

When the prophet Samuel was asked by Eli what the Lord had told Samuel, he "told him everything and hid nothing from him" (1 Samuel 3:18). In the normal course of business, we will be asked to commit to deadlines for projects and reports, and to follow through with delegated tasks. Part of our responsibility is to keep promises to our superiors.

Every promise we make to a boss is a promise we make to the Lord, so we need to mean what we say and follow through. When asked to arrive on time, improve our attitude, improve the quality of our work, or take other actions, we're being asked to make promises, and these are promises we need to keep.

When dealing with your boss, you would be wise to develop the same "count the cost" mentality that you use with customers. Instead of having you come up short on your commitments, your boss would probably rather be told what other work is on your plate; and if your plate is full, to give input about what can be delayed or deleted from your to-do list. Granted, at times you may be given unreasonable deadlines. But honesty is still the best policy when dealing with other people, and your boss will likely appreciate your honesty, rather than having you break your commitments.

Promises to Colleagues

Part of being a good team player is following through on commitments we make to colleagues and coworkers. Tom was a very effective salesman for a rubber hose company. But one of his weaknesses was that he continually failed to advise the accounting department when he negotiated special pricing with customers. As a result, many invoicing errors occurred. Correcting these errors not only cost the company additional time and expense in accounts receivable, but it also undermined customer relations and affected cash flow while all the disputed billings were sorted out.

When we keep promises to our coworkers, we build up goodwill. When our colleagues know that they can trust our word, they're much more open to helping us. Simple statements such as, "I'll send the file over today"; "I will let you know the number of vacations days you have this year by Friday"; and "I will process your expense report today," are all promises we need to keep.

Settling Obligations in a Timely Manner

Part of building integrity is settling our obligations in a timely manner. God told the nation of Israel through the prophet Jeremiah, "Now you have shrugged off your oath and defiled my name" (Jeremiah 34:16, NLT). As Christians in business, we need to understand that we dishonor the Lord whenever we fail to deliver on our promises.

Making payments on time is a key element of integrity. Negotiating the best possible payment terms is great, but after we make a purchase we are bound by the payment agreement, or by the fine print on the order form. Net ten days means that we pay in ten days, not thirty. I know one businessperson who was struggling financially, and would not place new orders until he believed he would be able to pay for it. Though at times it may be difficult for us to honor our commitments, the Lord will honor our integrity. I have seen other businesspeople order merchandise on credit, even though they know they are in deep financial trouble. Then they juggle orders between vendors to string out payments.

Buying on credit, whether business or personal, is the same as borrowing from your suppliers. King David writes, "The wicked borrow and never repay" (Psalm 37:21, NLT). When many business owners file bankruptcy, they leave their creditors in the dust. Anyone can experience a business failure, but we need to understand that failing to pay our bills is a sin. Fortunately, like any sin, we can confess it, repent, make restitution as possible, and allow the Lord to wipe our slate clean. Nevertheless, we have a responsibility to avoid sin in our lives, including failure to pay what we owe. A bankruptcy court might legally eliminate our debt, but it doesn't eliminate our sin.

Some obligations are not financial, but our responsibility to follow through in a timely manner is the same. Whether it's providing financial reports to the bank, issuing shareholder reports, or getting information to others as agreed, when we have made a commitment to do something by a certain date and time, we need to honor that commitment. A practical fact is that when we fail to provide information to the bank as agreed, we have violated our loan agreement, and the loan could be called immediately by the bank. One business had a loan from an investor for $50,000. The terms were that interest was due each quarter, net worth had to remain over $250,000, and an updated income statement and balance sheet was due by the tenth of each month. When the lender received the statements late for several months, they demanded immediate repayment of the $50,000 balance due. Because the borrower had failed to honor his commitments, he was forced to sell the business in order to pay off the loan.

When We Fail to Do What We Say

If we fail to honor our commitments for any reason, we need to start by confessing our failure to the Lord and to the offended party. King Solomon writes, "He who conceals his transgressions will not prosper, but he who confesses and forsakes them will find compassion" (Proverbs 28:13).

Customers react better when we apologize for our failure, or our organization's failure. A simple "I'm, sorry" goes a lot further than excuses like, "Gee, we had a rush of customers and just didn't get your order out." Excuses tell your customers that they are unimportant, and that you believe your problems are more important than your promises. A cop-out or a long story is not a confession. Confessions are best received when we acknowledge what we're sorry for and explain how we will avoid future problems. As King Solomon advised, confession is part one of the process, but part two is *forsaking our failure*. When we continually apologize for failures, our apologies lose their effectiveness. Customers will no longer believe what we say, because they can see that the underlying problem was never fixed. It may be that we have to change our processes to ensure future improvement.

After confession, we need to make amends and not ask our customer to bear the consequences of our failure. Solomon writes, "Fools mock at making amends for sin, but goodwill is found among the upright" (Proverbs 14:9, NIV).

Tim sold me two sport coats and promised that the alterations would be completed by Friday. I stopped by on Saturday, only to learn that there was a problem with the tailor and the jackets would not be ready for another few days. I expressed concern that I had not been called and would need to make another trip out of my way to retrieve the jackets. After apologizing, Tim immediately offered to drop the sport coats by my office, saving me a trip and cementing a solid relationship.

When I receive poor service, I ask the service person, "Are you expecting your customer to bear the consequences of your error?" I have learned to remain silent until I receive an answer. When it's our mistake, we should expect to assume responsibility and shoulder the consequences rather than foist the problem back on our customers. As Scripture instructs, we must make amends as needed. The positive aspect of every mistake is that when we absorb the loss, we are very motivated to improve in the future, and avoid future losses. Our customers will also be pleased, and they may even do more business with us than before.

Case Study: Honoring Commitments

Phil started Beeline Contracting eleven years ago, specializing in home remodeling. He had two employees—Bob, who worked full time, and Andrew, a retired fireman working part time. Phil's wife, Janelle, assisted by ordering supplies, scheduling appointments, doing office correspondence, and fielding telephone calls. Phil and Janelle made enough money to get by, but the business never grew and bills were paid paycheck to paycheck.

Then Phil landed a $200,000 contract for a retail store addition. The contract called for Beeline to start the job in two weeks and finish in three months, or a penalty of $800 per day would be assessed for late completion. Beeline received a $25,000 down payment, with the balance to be paid by a contractor's draw.

In order to start the store project on schedule, Phil called two other customers for whom he had agreed to do work and said he would be unable to do the jobs as agreed. Next, he made a list of supplies needed for the addition. But when Janelle placed the first order, she was told that all materials would need to be prepaid because of late payments on earlier jobs. The equipment rental place also refused to extend credit, citing past-due balances that often remained outstanding for six months. Some prepaid materials were ordered (using up the down payment), and other suppliers were found who were willing to extend 30-day credit terms, but their prices were higher.

Phil hired two temporary workers and told Andrew that he would need him to work full time until the job was done. Andrew reminded Phil that he had agreed to work only three days a week, and he had other plans for his off days. When Phil persisted, Andrew said that a deal was a deal and he would only work as promised and no more. Phil got angry and told Andrew to either work six days a week or leave. Andrew left, taking his experience with him, and Phil was forced to hire another temporary carpenter.

As the project went on, Phil fell behind schedule, which meant he received the contractor's draw slower than he had planned. Meanwhile, the higher material costs were eating away at his profit margin. When Janelle was told that no more supplies would be shipped until past-due bills were paid, Phil switched to other vendors. However, with orders now being juggled between several companies, there were several delays in receiving needed provisions.

Janelle expressed concern about the project schedule and cost overruns, but Phil kept saying it wasn't his fault, that the suppliers were unreasonable and the temporary help was unreliable. As time went by, he replaced each short-term crew member with another.

When the job was finally completed, it was 36 days late. When Phil met with the store owner, he explained his problems with higher-than-expected material costs, but the owner replied that Phil had agreed to a price, and that price must be honored. Furthermore, the owner assessed the $800-per-day penalty, meaning that Beeline would receive $28,800 less than the $200,000 original contract. Phil was outraged, insisting that the delays were not his fault. He said that he had worked night and day to finish the job and should be paid.

In total, Beeline lost $37,000 on the project, forcing Phil and Janelle to take out a second mortgage on their home. In addition, they gave up the $22,000 they would have made on the jobs that were canceled.

Questions:

- What past missteps help to create the disastrous project?
- When Phil and Janelle found themselves in trouble, what steps could they have taken to mitigate the loss?
- What biblical principles were violated by Beeline (and how many)?

CHAPTER 4

Sharing Decision-Making with Others

M any business leaders have confidence in themselves and their decisions. Self-assurance is important, but Solomon warns, "The way of a fool seems right to him, but a wise man listens to advice" (Proverbs 12:15, NIV). Throughout Scripture, we learn the benefits of seeking wise counsel and listening to the voice of others.

In a team-building exercise often used to demonstrate the value of group decisions, participants are asked to imagine that they have been shipwrecked on a deserted island. Everyone is given a list of 25 items and is told to choose ten to keep, based on their importance for survival on the island. After each person makes a list, the group members interact and agree on a common list of ten items to keep. The lists are then graded according to a standard list determined by a panel of survival experts. In every case, the group list turns out to be better than any individual's list. So, we know in principle that group decisions are better than decisions we make on our own, but we still must choose to include others in our decision-making processes.

Sharing Decision-Making with God

First of all, every decision should be shared with the Lord. King David writes, "The Lord says, 'I will guide you along the best pathway for your life. I will advise you and watch over you'" (Psalm 32:8, NLT). Asaph writes, "You guide me with your counsel" (Psalm 73:24, NLT). Isaiah refers to one of the names of the Lord as "Wonderful Counselor" (Isaiah 9:6).

When we ask the Lord for guidance, we must quietly and patiently wait for His answer. He may say yes, no, or wait. If we charge ahead without asking the Lord for guidance, we are acting on our own strength. We shouldn't then insist that the Lord bless our plans. Instead, we must be willing to respond to His plan. As we ask for guidance, the Lord will give us peace, not anxiety, as we move forward.

Sharing Decision-Making with Customers

Given that our customers support our businesses and pay our salaries, we should consider bringing customer input into our decision-making processes. The 3M Company has long recognized the value of customer input. Most of the innovative ideas they implement have come from customer feedback.

Matt runs a touristy art shop in Jerome, Arizona. Most stores in Jerome close at 5 P.M., after many of the daytime visitors have left town. While chatting with some of his customers, Matt heard several mention their frustration that there was nothing to do after all the shops closed. Some said they would like to stay in Jerome for dinner, but they didn't want to eat at five o'clock and they hated to waste an hour waiting. Others said they just left town when the sidewalks were rolled up.

With his location near several trendy eating places, Matt decided to stay open an extra hour in the evening. The result was a steady stream of customers who browsed while waiting for dinnertime. The hour between five and six soon became Matt's best sales time, all as a result of listening to his customers and responding to their feedback.

In the past, I serviced air freight customers who needed expedited service. We would gather together several import shipments and dispatch them for prompt delivery. One customer wanted extremely fast service twice a week. I explained that in order to meet his requirement, I would have to pay to have a delivery truck standing by when the air cargo was unloaded and cleared U.S. Customs, and then immediately dispatch that truck to the plant. I told him that the exclusive use of the truck and the waiting time would be expensive. My customer understood the costs and said that he still wanted the service, so we agreed on a price. Over time, several other customers requested and paid for this premium-level service.

How often have you heard, "I'm sorry, but this is how we do things," when you ask for something different, rather than, "What can we do to meet your needs?" As business owners and managers, we want to offer our customers a high level of service; however, a word of caution is in order before we decide whether we can accommodate special requests: We must make sure we have carefully counted the cost to ensure that we don't lose money and are able to deliver. If we want to be customer driven, we must open up the channels of communication.

Solomon noted, "Through presumption comes nothing but strife" (Proverbs 13:10). This principle certainly applies to our communications with customers. Instead of presuming that we know what our customers want, we must devise a system of regular feedback that works. Smart restaurant owners, for example, ask their regular customers what new items they might like to see added to the menu.

Coldstone Creamery's retail stores custom blend many delicious ice cream treats. Most of the great creations they offer were designed by customer feedback, rather than by extensive market research. As customers ordered similar combinations of ingredients, the stores added the new concoctions to the menu list. Customer-driven menus are just one of the reasons why Coldstone Creamery was named by *Entrepreneur* magazine as one of the fastest growing franchises in 2006. Taking time to ask our customers what they want—and to listen to what they say—keeps us connected to our greatest source of good ideas.

Sharing Decision-Making with Your Staff

Every day, great ideas flow from our employees. Owners and managers who believe they have nothing to learn from their staff should consider how King David managed his army: "Then David consulted with the captains of the thousands and the hundreds, even with every leader" (1 Chronicles 13:1). Considering the size of David's army, that was a lot of people to ask. We will gain important information we need to keep our business intact.

Get into the habit of asking your employees questions, and don't be defensive when they give you suggestions that you don't like; otherwise, you'll close off the pipeline for future ideas. If an idea seems harebrained, ask for more information: "How would that work?" or "How would that save money?" or "How would that affect customers (or another department)?" The key is to encourage dialogue, participation, and understanding. Some of your staff may not communicate as effectively as you do, so help them out. Solomon advises, "A plan in the heart of a man is like deep water, but a man of understanding draws it out" (Proverbs 20:5).

Sam was an expert tool maker and made some great suggestions that enhanced the company's products, but sometimes he would get caught up in an idea and go on at some length about all the possible variations he could imagine. His manager learned to listen patiently as Sam explained his ideas, and that patience was generally rewarded with useful product or process improvements.

When you ask your employees for an opinion or feedback, you demonstrate your respect for them. We all like to be asked what we think—just look at the success of *American Idol*; viewers love to vote for their favorite singers. Likewise, your employees like to be asked for their input. One word of caution, though:

Don't ask if you don't care, because asking and not caring about the response, is worse than not asking at all.

One good question to regularly ask your employees is, "What can I do to assist you in your tasks?" You may learn from your sales staff that the credit department is slow in reviewing and approving credit applications, thus giving you an opportunity to intervene and help fix the logjam. One time I heard from my staff that the copy machines were jamming constantly. After reviewing the situation, I ordered several replacement copiers to help improve productivity.

When making decisions that will affect your staff, solicit their input to help you avoid mistakes and make the best choices. If someone tells you, "I don't think this new policy will work," follow up to find out why. A few well-chosen questions can help you differentiate between cases where the change is being resisted for no reason, and times where the objection is based on legitimate concerns. Sometimes your employees just need to hear more about how the changes will enhance their jobs. If a counter clerk, for example, expresses concern that a new computer system will take an extra sixty seconds to process each order, you can explain how the new system will automatically update inventory and prepare reorder lists, saving time and money overall. When your staff understands the logic and reasons behind your decisions, they can be more supportive.

Sharing Decision-Making with Your Boss

Your boss is another person with whom you should share decisions. We're sometimes reluctant to go "up the ladder" with decisions we feel we should make on our own. Of course, we need to exercise some discretion and not run to the person in charge for input on every little issue, but there are times when obtaining feedback from our superiors is prudent. As the apostle Paul writes, "We request of you, brethren, that you appreciate those who diligently labor among you, and have charge over you in the Lord and give you instruction" (1

Thessalonians 5:12). You can express appreciation and respect for your boss by asking for his or her advice on difficult issues.

One CEO said, "Bring me your problems early and you will find me a partner in working through a solution; bring me your disasters later and you will find me as a judge." Bosses, as a rule, don't like surprises, so when you're facing a difficult situation, bring your boss on board early and eliminate unpleasant surprises. Early in my career, I gained a lot of insight by consulting with my supervisor when I was having trouble managing a particular person. The advice I received not only helped me to resolve the issue with my staff member, but it also kept me from having to learn the hard way.

Ask your boss what types of issues you should discuss with him or her, and what issues you should handle independently. Most managers are in their positions based on their experience and good judgment; therefore, you should use your own good judgment in deciding when to draw on your boss' expertise and experience.

Some people like to say that it's easier to ask forgiveness than permission for some actions. But although we will all make mistakes and errors of judgment from time to time, we need to be responsible to understand and adhere to company policy. At one time I worked for a boss I knew would not approve of certain purchases. Several times, I intentionally waited until he was on vacation before placing my orders. After the third time, he rightly chastised me for working around his approval process. He reminded me that my authority during his absence was for urgent needs, not for circumventing the system. And he was right.

Sharing Decision-Making with Colleagues

The prophet Isaiah writes, "Let us review the situation together..." (Isaiah 43:26, NLT). Because our work naturally affects other people in the company, we must develop the habit of asking our colleagues for feedback. We need to avoid dumping our work and our problems onto other staff members.

Sarah, who worked for a wholesale distributor in their order-entry department, sometimes failed to process orders the same day, as required by company standards. As a result, the shipping department often needed to place a rush on shipments to comply with the 48-hour shipping service requirement. Sarah was unaware of the extra work and expense she was causing other people. Finally, the shipping manager met with Sarah, explained the situation, and asked that future orders be processed on time. If the problem persisted, the shipping manager would have to contact Sarah's manager. Fortunately, the problem was resolved by talking directly to Sarah.

When we decide to change systems or procedures, we should consider how the change will affect others in the organization. Rather than waiting for a bomb to go off, we should proactively meet with the other affected parties and explain the changes.

Sue, a credit manager, intended to introduce a new credit application with far greater detail than the old form. The sales and operations staff would have to spend a lot more time walking new customers through the process. Upon review, it was determined that the additional information was needed for only ten percent of the new customers—those whose credit was not well established. Instead of insisting that every new client fill out the long form, Sue changed her plans so that only those customers who fit the higher-risk profile were asked to complete the extra application. The result of Sue's interaction with the sales and operations staff was a far better system.

Sharing Decision-Making with Outside Counselors

At times, every business leader needs to develop and utilize outside counselors. King Solomon said, "Where there is no guidance the people fall, but in abundance of counselors there is victory" (Proverbs 11:14). Although Solomon was the wisest person who ever lived, he understood the need for additional counsel. Based on our particular business, we need to determine the type of outside help we need.

Sooner or later, every business needs the assistance of an attorney, accountant, or other specialist. Take time to research candidates. Ask friends for referrals, and look for specialists who have experience in your field. When you need to evict a tenant for nonpayment of rent, you don't want your attorney to have to research the process; you need someone who is up to speed on local tenancy laws. Likewise, check out accountants who are familiar with your type of business, and who have clients of similar size. An accounting firm that works primarily with large clients may not be well equipped to serve a small business. Likewise, if most of their clients are small businesses, they may lack the experience to handle more complex issues. An accountant whose practice is focused on tax returns may not be available during tax season, so keep those kinds of issues in mind.

As your business grows, you may need other specialists or consultants to help you with human resources, taxes, construction, business planning, or technical support. Connie, the owner of a printing company, fired several people without first getting professional counsel. She didn't want to spend $500 to consult with a human resources expert who could have advised her on the lawful method for terminating employees. The unfortunate result was a lawsuit for unlawful dismissal and a $50,000 judgment against her—a very expensive lesson.

Don't wait until you have a pressing need before you start looking for outside counselors. Anticipate your needs and arrange your contact list before you need the help. Be sure to check references to ensure that you have qualified people lined up as needed.

Sharing Decision-Making with Friends and Family

Asking your parents for counsel can be a wise move, even if they don't know your business well. They probably know you very well and want what's best for you. King Solomon confirmed this truth when he wrote, "Hear, my son, your father's instruction and do not forsake your mother's teaching"

(Proverbs 1:8). Asking for your parents' advice, and giving weight to their counsel, is a mark of wisdom.

Asking knowledgeable and experienced friends for advice can also be wise. Whenever I buy a car, I ask several of my friends who are car nuts for ideas and to confirm my thoughts. Businesspeople with more experience than you have can be a great help, and accountability business groups, when available, are also valuable.

Don't Let Pride Keep You from Seeking Counsel

Several factors keep us from seeking counsel, and pride is number one on the list. Solomon writes, "Pride leads to disgrace, but with humility comes wisdom" (Proverbs 11:2, NLT). As humans, we naturally want to go our own way. Every time we stop and ask for help or counsel, we may feel constrained. But it's better to humble ourselves and gain the benefit of wise counsel, than to charge ahead on our own and come to disgrace.

Sometimes, we just don't want to ask. For example, when I would ask a former boss to approve spending for something, I knew I would meet with resistance. Part of what felt like resistance to me was my boss' perfectly appropriate expectation that I justify the expense. If the item was not in the budget, he would always ask me, "If we spend money over here to make the purchase you want, where do you propose that we cut spending to offset the expense?" Even though these conversations were uncomfortable for me, they were necessary and productive. Still, I would have rather just run off and done my own thing.

Often people will come to me for counsel about whether they should start a new business. Half the time, my answer is no, and I explain the reasons why I don't think they should move forward. Nearly everyone goes ahead anyway, and most of the time they fail. I've learned that what they really want from me is my blessing on the path they've already decided to follow. What they don't want is counsel that runs counter to their desires. "Pride leads to disgrace, but with humility comes wisdom."

Another problem we have is that we don't like to be overruled. As the saying goes, "My mind is made up; don't confuse me with the facts." When King Solomon's son Rehoboam sought counsel, he was told, "If you will be kind to these people and please them and give them a favorable answer, they will always be your servants. But Rehoboam rejected the advice the elders gave him" (2 Chronicles 10:7-8, NIV). He rejected the voice of experience and listened to his friends instead. As a result, he lost half of his kingdom. Rehoboam, like many of us, wanted to listen only to people who agreed with him. The results were disastrous.

Finally, we may be so anxious we don't want to take the time to stop and ask for advice. Solomon writes, "Enthusiasm without knowledge is no good; haste makes mistakes" (Proverbs 19:2, NLT). Peter wanted to open a plumbing business. He had fifteen years of experience and believed he was ready. Due to his limited knowledge of accounting, he was advised by a friend to work out a bookkeeping system in advance. However, he ignored his friend's advice and plowed ahead with his business plan. As a result, within one year, he owed $15,000 in taxes and was $40,000 in debt. His books were a disaster because he regularly misplaced invoices and he didn't understand how to use the accounting package he had purchased. It wasn't long before he was forced into bankruptcy.

Most of us would like to gain wisdom without having to ask. When we seek advice, we are admitting our need for help, and acknowledging that we don't have all the answers. Just as when we turn to God, confess our sins, and make Jesus the Lord of our lives, we acknowledge our need for salvation. (If you don't already have a relationship with Jesus Christ and would like to, please turn to page 193 for some wise counsel.) Let's face it, nobody, short of God Himself, has all the answers. So let's set aside our pride and seek the wise counsel we need in order to be successful.

Case Study: Ignoring Red Flags

For ten years, Tom Bailey had owned and operated Green Mountain, a heating and cooling business in Vermont. Over the past three years, his sales had remained steady, but increasing costs had eroded his profit margin and he was now losing money. As his cash flow tightened, he was able to deposit less money into the family checking account, causing anxiety for his wife, June.

His accountant told him he was heading for trouble, but Tom replied, "I have had bumpy patches before, and have always gotten through. I just need to work harder and keep going."

Then a large business opportunity arose. Birch Acres, a building company, was developing a major new subdivision of two thousand homes. Tom was invited to bid on the project. Although he knew that Birch Acres had a history of financial problems, Tom decided to enter a bid.

An experienced businessman at church cautioned Tom to be careful, noting that Birch Acres had left subcontractors hanging in the past and had hurt many innocent parties. Still, Tom decided to proceed.

In order to take on the job, Tom needed an additional $100,000 in operating capital. After warning him about Birch Acres' reputation, the bank agreed to approve the loan if Tom would sign a personal guarantee, using his home as collateral. June was very uncomfortable about signing the personal guarantee, but after strongly expressing her concerns, she finally agreed.

Tom's accountant expressed concern that the bid was too low, and that Tom would not be able to increase prices if the cost of construction materials increased. He deemed the project "risky."

Over dinner one night, Tom and June shared the opportunity and concerns with his parents, who were retired.

Both parents expressed concern that the project would cause strain on the business and the family.

Despite all the red flags from his advisors, Tom signed a contract and started the work. Three months into the project, Hurricane Katrina struck, causing an immediate spike in material costs. When Tom asked Birch Acres for a price increase to offset the cost of materials, they told him that the original contract must be honored, and that any material increases were his problem, not theirs.

As the project continued, the progress payments started coming in late, causing Tom to go back to the bank for another $75,000. Tom's friend at church suggested he take a harder line with the builder, refusing to do more work until he was paid for what he had done. Tom was afraid that if he took that position, he would lose the business altogether. His friend replied, "The only thing worse than losing the business is doing the work and not getting paid."

Three months later, with payments lagging behind and material costs continuing to increase, Tom filed bankruptcy, nearly $300,000 in debt. He and June lost their house and their IRA account, forcing them to start over financially.

Questions:
- Did Tom consult the Lord?
- How many advisors counseled against the deal?
- Did Tom take any action or further review as a result of his feedback?
- Given the counsel he received, could Tom have gone forward with Birch Acres by negotiating different terms?
- What changes could have saved him from bankruptcy?

CHAPTER 6

Accepting Responsibility for Actions and Results

Most of us don't like to admit our failures. We're quick to claim credit for victories and successes, and even quicker to blame other people, bad luck, or unfortunate circumstances when things go wrong. We take the lazy way out, rather than accept responsibility, because we don't want to invest the time and effort it will take to figure out how and why the problem occurred. King Solomon writes, "The lazy man is full of excuses. 'I can't go to work!' he says. 'If I go outside, I might meet a lion in the street and be killed!'" (Proverbs 22:13, LB). Accepting full responsibility requires that we humbly look at ourselves, rather than blame others, and then do the hard work of fixing the problems.

Many businesspeople today seem to have invented a new type of math: A mistake + a good explanation = an acceptable result. Somehow, the storyteller believes that the explanation (or the excuse) changes the outcome. In reality, however, a bad result is a bad result, regardless of how you got there.

Scripture asks, "Shall a talkative man be acquitted?" (Job 11:2). Excuses and defensiveness only get in the way of solving problems. They keep us from understanding what is going wrong, and what is going *right*.

Developing a Complete Understanding of Reality

The first step in accepting responsibility for results is an unrelenting search for the truth. This requires objective thinking. The apostle Paul writes, "Refuse foolish and ignorant speculations, knowing that they produce quarrels" (2 Timothy 2:23). When something fails to work well, or takes a dive, we need to ask what went wrong, and why. Only when these questions have been asked and answered can we consider an action plan for making progress.

James owned River Construction, a building company specializing in remodeling and additions. Over the years, he had built the company up to where they had six full-time work crews out in the field. James wanted to expand his business further by entering the market for building custom homes in the $400,000 to $750,000 range. He hired a marketing company and started advertising. Before long, he was receiving an average of two bid requests per week. However, after several weeks he had only been able to land one job.

When James complained to the marketing company about the lack of business, they explained that a response rate of two bid requests per week was a good result for the size of his advertising budget. But James wasn't satisfied.

Frustrated, he hired another marketing company and tried another advertising campaign—with similar results. Then he tried a third marketing company, and again nothing changed. He assumed that the problem was with the marketing companies, and not his fault.

Because James refused to look beyond his advertising efforts, he failed to understand the bigger picture, which would have saved him a lot of grief and money. First, he was accustomed to pitching jobs between $50,000 and $100,000, largely to families needing more room in their existing homes. But customers who were building large custom homes required a different approach—an approach that James failed to understand completely. As a result, the way he presented his company's capabilities turned off these custom home buyers.

Second, James was used to the higher profit margins that went along with smaller remodeling jobs. When he bid on custom home projects, he calculated his regular margin, not realizing that the added markup made many of his bids uncompetitive.

When sales are disappointing, we need to candidly assess why we are falling short, and not jump to conclusions. In James' case, if he had carefully studied his prospects, he would have learned that most of the referrals he received went on to build their homes with other builders. The problem was not that he wasn't receiving good leads, it was his inability to convert those good leads into business. A more effective plan would have included following up on lost bids to determine why the business was placed elsewhere. With a little extra effort, James could have easily learned that many potential customers saw his bids as high, and therefore stopped considering him as a builder.

Obtaining Feedback from Different Viewpoints

Part of developing a true sense of reality is obtaining feedback from as many perspectives as possible. We each have our own view of the world, through which we filter everything we see. We cannot escape from how we see the world, but we can broaden our perspective by obtaining feedback from different points of view. But first we must understand ourselves, our past experiences, and how our point of view affects how we see events in our lives and in our businesses.

Mike had been burned a few times early in his business career when deadbeats failed to pay outstanding invoices. As a result, he developed a tight credit policy, which he summed up with the phrase, "In God we trust; all others pay cash." Although this approach eliminated his bad debt expense, it made it difficult for many creditworthy customers to do business with him. Mike blamed the customers for not being willing to pay cash up front, and by allowing his past experience to cloud his vision, he lost a lot of business that he could have had. Rather than retreat from credit sales entirely, he could have taken a step back, reevaluated and improved his credit-approval processes, and done a better job of weeding out the deadbeats from the creditworthy customers. By relying entirely on his own experience and perspective, he hurt his business.

King Solomon writes, "Without consultation, plans are frustrated, but with many counselors they succeed" (Proverbs 15:22). We need to develop feedback from different people and different viewpoints.

Customers are a great source of feedback—if you listen. Have you ever raised a service issue with a company, only to be told, "Nobody else has complained," or "We always do a great job," and have your complaint ignored? At my import/export company, a customer called me and complained that our transit time on sea shipments from the Philippines was slow and unacceptable. My belief was that most of our transit times were within our standard terms, and I was confident we were providing first-class service. Still, I agreed to look into the situation. After digging around a bit, I learned that our agent in Manila wasn't issuing documents until after the freight was received. If I calculated our service time based on when the customer delivered the merchandise to the warehouse, we were performing poorly, but according to the date on the documents, we were delivering on time. Only after understanding the depth of the problem—a problem surfaced by a customer—could the true issue be addressed and fixed.

In another case, I entrusted an employee named Derrick with highly confidential information. I received feedback from others that Derrick was consistently leaking information. Because I held Derrick in high regard, I was inclined to believe that the leak came from someone else. I allowed my opinion of Derrick to cloud my objectivity. I continued to keep Derrick in the loop while emphasizing the importance of confidentiality. Still, the leaks continued, and I paid a price in lost business. Finally, I shared a particular piece of information only with Derrick, and when that morsel leaked out, I had to accept the reality that Derrick was not trustworthy and my confidence had been misplaced. Though I needed to hold Derrick accountable for his actions, I also had to accept responsibility for my own poor judgment, and for being slow to verify the facts.

Jefferson Florist in Detroit was known for its exquisite—but expensive—floral arrangements. The quality of their flowers was impeccable and they had an incredible selection of imported stock from around the world. The problem was that Jefferson's prices were twenty to thirty percent higher than the competition, and many customers would not pay a premium price, even for better quality and selection. Sales slumped for several years while Tony, the owner, continued to insist that quality and selection were the hallmarks of his business and he wouldn't change. He insisted that customers had to understand the value and cost of quality.

Unfortunately, the market would not support the higher prices. Even when customers agreed the fresher flowers lasted longer, they were unwilling to pay significantly more for them. Tony got stuck with his view that high-quality flowers would sell, while in reality his business was shrinking. He blamed market conditions, uneducated customers, cut-rate supermarket competitors, and Internet marketers for the decline in his business. Finally, after 35 years in business, Tony had to close the doors.

Small businesses are not the only ones to get caught up in narrow-minded thinking. A key reality is that most large Wall Street mergers fail to meet shareholder expectations. Though some work well, more than half fail to meet the stated objectives. When disappointing earnings are released, the CEOs will often talk about different market conditions, how the expected synergies failed to produce, or how a reduction in costs could not be achieved. Unfortunately, when CEOs and corporate boards fail to understand and clearly articulate, how and why their mergers failed to work as planned, their companies are likely to plunge into other unsatisfactory ventures. Regardless of the reasons for disappointing results, as business leaders we must start by accepting personal responsibility.

Responsibility Cannot Be Delegated

Part of being in leadership is the reality that we cannot escape responsibility for work that goes on under our authority. King Solomon writes, "Don't try to disclaim responsibility by saying you didn't know about it" (Proverbs 24:12, LB). We may want to evade responsibility for actions taken by others, but Scripture is clear that we cannot. Though we must delegate work and decisions, we are still on the hook for the ultimate results.

Create the Right Culture

First, we have a responsibility to create a business culture that is ethical and honorable, starting with our personal example. If the leaders arrive late, take long lunches, or take extra time off, why should they be surprised if the employees start easing back? If leaders shade the truth with customers, or know that others in the organization do but allow it to go on, they're creating a culture of dishonesty. In some companies, the standard seems to be "anything goes, as long as you don't get caught, embarrassed, or break the law."

As a leader, one of your most important responsibilities is to envision the business culture you desire, and then strive to build that culture.

A magazine salesman inflated the circulation numbers of his magazine at times to gain advertising sales. The CEO was aware of the situation, but he was content to look the other way because he was happy with the increased sales. After receiving bonuses based on his sales performance, the salesman not only continued to inflate the numbers, but pushed the erroneous information to more customers. When several advertisers who had experienced disappointing results filed a complaint that the circulation numbers on which their advertising rates were based were fraudulent, the owner claimed he had never lied or misrepresented the numbers. He pinned the total responsibility on the salesman, and then fired him. In reality, the boss had created the culture that resulted in the malfeasance.

Bob was given a company car as part of his employment package. He was an alcoholic and often drove under the influence of alcohol. His supervisor knew that Bob would stop for a few drinks on his way home each night, but he failed to confront Bob, even though he knew that driving under the influence was against company policy and exposed the company to increased liability. After ten years on the job, Bob had an accident that damaged the car and injured him and two others, who sued both Bob and the company. The company tried to claim that they had a drinking policy in place, and thus were not negligent in allowing Bob to drive a company vehicle. However, when testimony established that Bob's drinking and driving was well know to the company's managers, and they had not taken steps to stop it, the award for damages was increased. Had management confronted the issue and either insisted the practice stop or take away the company vehicle, liability would have been avoided.

Under current law, workplaces are required to be free of sexual harassment. When leaders tolerate off-color remarks, jokes, or demeaning talk, a culture is established where harassment is okay, and we should not be surprised with the results.

Honesty is a key part of culture that must be built into every business. When we set the standard that we will never lie to a customer, and that we expect total honesty from our staff, that is the first step. We are responsible for the conduct of our staff. Some people may want to tell "little white lies" to get off the hook with a customer, but when we take a hard line that the truth must be part of every conversation, we establish the culture for truth. I established a policy that lying to a customer was grounds for dismissal, and I discharged a manager after verifying that he had lied several times to customers. Firing the manager sent a message to the organization that was clearly understood by all.

Create the Right Instructions

We need to assume responsibility for effective training and ensure that training is followed. One of the best training methods I've discovered is a three-step process:

1. Do the task yourself while the newcomer watches.

2. Have the new employee do the task while you watch and give instructions.

3. Have the newcomer do the work under some level of supervision.

Just instructing someone and then walking away doesn't suffice. We need to set up a system to ensure that the work is done right every time. As it says in the Bible, "Moses inspected the work and saw that they had done it just as the Lord commanded" (Exodus 39:43, NIV). Moses wisely knew that if the work was not done well, he couldn't tell the Lord, "Gee, it's not my fault; the worker just failed to follow instructions." Our staff's performance will only be as good as our training system and follow-up.

Enforce the Responsibility to Hire and Delegate

Part of a manager's responsibility is to hire a team that will be effective. We must develop the skill to become effective evaluators of talent so that we can hire the right team. When our employees perform poorly or inefficiently, we need to evaluate the process by which we built the staff and determine how we can improve in the future.

I have had managers try to evade responsibility when a member of their staff messed up and they didn't know about it. My response is always the same: "You hired that person, he or she reports to you, and you have the responsibility to ensure that the work performed is up to standards."

Confess When Appropriate

Confession is the beginning of improvement. King Solomon writes, "He who conceals his transgressions will not prosper, but he who confesses and forsakes them will find compassion" (Proverbs 28:13). Effective confession states what we are sorry for and what we could have done differently.

We need to differentiate between events that require confession and those that do not. When we fall short in our product or service delivery we need to confess our underperformance. In other cases when we have delivered as promised but the customer seems dissatisfied or confused, we may need to just be open to receive and learn from their feedback. Or they may need some issues clarified. But there is no need to apologize if we haven't done anything wrong. At times, looking back, we do not see that we would have acted any differently if we had it to do over again. Not every move is going to work, regardless of how well thought out it is.

Being in a position of responsibility does not guarantee we will be successful. A ship's captain may be responsible to evade submarine attack, but he may be torpedoed anyway. Though the captain is responsible for the ship, he cannot control every circumstance. His responsibility is to maintain the prescribed speed and course, and to take evasive action when under attack.

When we confess, we need to move beyond a mere apology and make restitution as necessary. Confession will strengthen our relationships, especially when we confirm what we will do differently in the future. Confession should be quick, and public if necessary. Jesus said, "Settle matters quickly with your adversary" (Matthew 5:25, NIV). The sooner we confess and make amends, the sooner we can go forward on the right foot.

I can give you a personal example of learning responsibility from an incident that occurred when I was behind the wheel. I used to be an aggressive driver who was often in a hurry to get places. I was a master at pushing the limits without collecting traffic tickets. For example, I would exceed the speed limit, but not by enough to attract attention. I was the first car off the line when the light changed, and I was quick to change to a better lane.

On my regular route to work, I entered a freeway ramp from a street just past an intersection. The ramp was on the right side of the road, and there was a traffic light at the intersection. One morning, a truck was waiting in the right lane at the light, so I pulled up in the left lane. When the light changed, I immediately hit the gas so I could pull in front of the truck and enter the freeway.

What I couldn't see until I pulled ahead of the truck was that a car had run the red light and was approaching from the right. It was too late to stop, and a collision occurred. The other driver was ticketed, and the accident was technically not my fault, but upon reflection, I knew that my aggressive driving was a key factor. By accepting responsibility, even when I was officially not at fault, I was able to alter my driving and become a safer driver.

Case Study: The Call Center

Mitch was the assistant manager of a telephone call center that serviced thirty customers, mostly catalog companies and television advertising companies. Depending on the expected call volume, between thirty and 115 telephone operators were on duty at a given time. The call center took orders in both Spanish and English, so many employees were bilingual, and for some, Spanish was their first language.

Mitch was responsible for hiring staff, managing the supervisors, scheduling shifts, training new employees, and maintaining quality control. Connie, the newly promoted call center manager, was responsible for budgeting, equipment maintenance, innovation, and operating efficiency. Mitch, who had been in his position for seven years, was unhappy that he had not been offered the manager's job, even though he had received excellent annual reviews. The company paid annual bonuses based on profits and how each manager met key target goals, and Mitch had received the maximum bonus the last three years.

Mitch was a great interviewer and hired well, but he delegated the hiring of Spanish-speaking employees to bilingual supervisors. At times, Connie helped in the hiring process, given her excellent Spanish skills (a skill shared by the previous manager). Training was conducted in both English and Spanish, with Connie conducting the Spanish training and Mitch the English.

Mitch worked well with the supervisors in documenting the efficiency of each operator, and he had a carefully developed plan in place to assist each supervisor in performance improvement. He had also designed a program to enhance training on new products being sold by the call center. His system, which had been adopted by the company's fifteen other call centers nationwide, assisted the operators to more effectively answer product-specific questions.

Despite Mitch's superior administrative skills, however, a number of employees had complained to Connie that he was a poor listener and never took personal requests into account when schedules were set. He also had a temper and would occasionally unleash a public tirade against employees who made mistakes. Connie was very good at smoothing ruffled feathers.

Connie met with Mitch and told him that he would need to take direct responsibility for all interviewing, hiring, and training—not just with English-speaking employees, and that the corporate office was asking for a five percent reduction in the error rate on customer orders. Mitch felt that Connie was unnecessarily focusing on his weaknesses, and his anger displays to staff became more frequent.

Questions:
- Do you believe that Mitch's former boss did an effective job of management development?

- Should Mitch be pleased because he received a bonus each year?
- What counsel would you give Mitch at this time?
- How should Connie manage the current situation with Mitch?

CHAPTER   7

Judging Employees Fairly

Anytime we hire staff, or have people reporting to us, we are in a position to judge them. Some owners and managers are reluctant to judge other people, referring to Matthew 7:1, "Do not judge so that you will not be judged." It's important, however, not to ignore the rest of what Jesus says: "For in the way you judge, you will be judged; and by your standard of measure, it will be measured to you" (Matthew 7:2). So, it isn't so much that we shouldn't exercise judgment or discernment, but that we must judge fairly and carefully.

If we take a position that we are never to judge, what do we do when an employee steals or fails to come to work on time? If we decide to draw the line at some point, we become judges. The only remaining question is how will we judge? Jesus said, "Stop judging by mere appearances, and make a right judgment" (John 7:24, NIV). Making the *right* judgment is key. To do this requires an orderly process.

A leader with integrity understands that good stewardship requires effective management of employees and all resources, which in turn entails the exercise of good judgment. Paul writes, "I pray that ... you will keep on growing in knowledge and understanding" (Philippians 1:9, NLT). But he also writes, "It takes only one wrong person among you to infect all the others." (Galatians 5:9, LB). Our goal, as stewards of our companies, is to help our employees grow and improve, while eliminating those whose lack of integrity will detract from the business.

Establish Clear Expectations

First, we must establish clear on-the-job expectations. How can we judge fairly unless we have been clear about what we expect? Governments pass laws to establish which activities are legal, and which are not. Who would want to live under an authority that could decide what a crime is on the spot?

We need to start with clear, written expectations. "Moses carefully wrote down all the Lord's instructions" (Exodus 24:4 NLT), because he wisely knew that he and the people could not remember every detail from memory. Likewise, our employees will not remember everything unless we write it down. They cannot be held accountable for what they do not know.

Each position should have a clear job description. When hiring, a good practice is to hand a copy of the job description to the prospective employee and ask, "Can you do this job? Do you *want* to do this job? What skills do you have to be effective in this position?" When you start with a clear job description, you establish the scope of the position. For example, a receptionist's job description might include the following duties:

- Answering the telephone
- Accurately directing calls
- Accurately taking complete messages
- Greeting and directing visitors
- Filing papers
- Placing and following up on equipment service calls
- Preparing correspondence.

The more clear and complete our job descriptions are, the more effectively we can hire, and the more likely we are to avoid the disappointment of a bad hiring decision.

Additionally, we need to establish clear job performance standards. Any business owner or manager must be able to define what good work is. This may sound simple, but I've had many clients who could not adequately define how staff productivity and performance should be measured. Sales performance is easier to judge. Each salesperson can be given a quota for obtaining new business, and they either reach the goal or they don't. But every job should have some quantifiable, measurable function. These measurable factors can then be defined as job standards. Starting work on time is an obvious standard. Quality of work, customer response, and productivity also can and must be quantified.

If work expectations are not put in writing, then a manager's feedback becomes just an opinion. Until we have established clear expectations, and have communicated those expectations to our staff, we do not have a reasonable starting place for judging their performance. Without clear and measurable performance standards, our employees will be "like sheep [that] have gone astray, each...turned to his own way" (Isaiah 53:6, NIV). Our job as managers is to keep our sheep from going astray, while bringing them back into the fold when they do wander.

Provide Effective Feedback

Providing effective feedback is a key to improving employee performance. King Solomon writes, "In the end, people appreciate honest criticism far more than flattery" (Proverbs 28:23, NLT). Several principles will help us provide effective feedback.

Cultivate a Style of Direct
and Effective Communication
Before you confront an employee about a lapse in performance, first confirm the facts of what happened. Moses writes, "Never convict anyone...on the testimony of one witness"

(Deuteronomy 19:15, LB). When you confirm what happened, the employee becomes the second witness. Most of the time, when we ask quickly after an event occurs, we receive correct and truthful feedback.

Ask your employee what happened, and allow a moment of silence, if necessary. When you ask, "Did you ship the merchandise to Colonial Supply yesterday, as promised?" wait for an answer. Ask for a confirmation of the facts; don't allow a lot of chatter. If you ask about the shipment, and start receiving a long answer about how busy the department was yesterday, focus again on the original question: "Did the shipment go out yesterday, yes, or no?"

Follow up your fact-finding questions with a statement of the results of the miscue: "Because the shipment was sent late, the customer canceled the order," or, "We needed to absorb overnight shipping charges because we failed to ship on the promised date." Reinforcing the consequences, or possible consequences, with your staff will help them understand the importance of effective performance. Also, you can take this opportunity to refer the employee back to the job description and performance standards, by saying, "Our standard is that every shipment must be sent on time, unless a supervisor approves the delay."

If you're addressing a performance issue that you directly observed, state what you saw using specific, factual words, not vague general statements. Instead of saying, "You messed up with that customer," address the specific behavior. For example, "Losing your temper with that customer was unacceptable. Regardless of how hot a customer gets, you have a responsibility to keep your cool and not fire back."

For employees who have trouble getting to work on time, instead of saying, "You are always late," be specific: "You have been late to work three times this week and eight times this month."

When addressing employee mistakes, instead of saying, "Your sloppy work costs us," again, be specific: "By failing to correctly measure three customer window openings this month, we lost $600."

By keeping your tone objective and your facts straight, you will keep the discussion objective.

Separate opinion from fact by avoiding phrases like "I think," "I feel," "I consider," or "I assume." Definitive statements, such as "I observed," "the customer called and said...," "the order was delivered late," or "yesterday six orders were shipped late," remove the specter of doubt from the discussion and don't encourage debate. Specific statements require us to understand explicitly what happened and to keep the focus on the issue. If the discussion degenerates into how we *feel*, the focus has been lost. Managing with integrity requires us to focus on objective fact, rather than subjective feelings.

Stick to essentials by avoiding preferences that just don't matter. For example, an accounting department may require hand entries to be made in ink to stop possible fraudulent changes in the future. But insisting that blue ink be used instead of black is pointless, unless you have a sound reason beyond the fact that you like blue ink. When employees understand the reasons behind our directions, they will cooperate more willingly.

Act Quickly

When performance issues arise, act quickly to resolve them. Solomon writes, "When the sentence for a crime is not quickly carried out, the hearts of the people are filled with schemes to do wrong" (Ecclesiastes 8:11, NIV). Time will erode even the best memory. Facts that can be easily confirmed on the spot may become clouded and more difficult to confirm later. Evidence may be lost, making the facts more difficult to confirm.

Time also allows rationalization and defensiveness to develop. For example, if you are on the telephone talking with a client when a customer enters the store, and two service employees are discussing last night's football game instead of waiting on the customer, you should address the situation as soon as the customer has left and you are off the phone.

If, within a few moments you ask, "Did you see the customer enter the store? Did you see the customer walk up to the counter? Did you see the customer waiting at the counter? What were you discussing while the customer was waiting?" you will open up the platform for improvement. With the incident still fresh, you can say, "In the future, when a customer enters the store, you need to discontinue your personal conversation and attend to the customer." If you wait until tomorrow to follow up, your employees might say, "What customer? What conversation?" and the opportunity to correct future actions will be lost.

Problems also have a way of festering if not resolved quickly, which can damage your business in countless ways. If the roof leaks, you know that the damage will only get worse until the leak is fixed. It's the same way with "leaks" in employee performance. If the counter clerks continue to ignore customers, how many will simply walk out of the store rather than going to the trouble of finding another employee to help them? The sooner an issue is addressed and fixed, the faster you will see improvement.

Moreover, unless you identify substandard work and unacceptable behavior, your staff will believe that everything is okay. Silence gives sanction to sin, and encourages more of the same. But even if we admonish an employee in private, we send a message to the rest of the staff. Word has a way of getting out.

Provide Regular Feedback

On-the-spot feedback is important, but we also need to establish a regular process for feedback. Jesus said, "These things I have spoken to you so that you may be kept from stumbling" (John 16:1). Establish fixed evaluation or feedback times—and then stick to them. Don't forget to give positive feedback as well as correction.

A common issue for many business leaders is finding the time to prepare and conduct effective performance reviews. But if we say, and believe, that our employees are our most important asset, then we must make timely feedback a priority. If we promise to hold annual reviews by December 1 and then miss that deadline, we have failed to honor our word. The absence of timely reviews is a major complaint among employees. Solomon writes, "Hope deferred makes the heart sick, but desire fulfilled is a tree of life" (Proverbs 13:12). Because performance reviews go hand-in-hand with anticipated raise opportunities, putting off reviews lowers company morale.

Use Good Judgment
Effective management requires us to use good judgment about when to confront issues. Not every situation requires immediate intervention. As the apostle Paul instructs, "Avoid foolish controversies ... and arguments and quarrels about the law, because these are unprofitable and useless (Titus 3:9, NIV). Several key principles can help us decide when a concern ought to be addressed.

1. When a situation repeats itself, it requires action, even if the issue is minor. Repeated problems that go unaddressed can grow into bigger problems that are harder to solve. Bill, an employee in a business office answered the phone using only his first name. His supervisor preferred that employees give their full name when answering the phone. Although it wasn't a major issue, the supervisor mentioned it to Bill, who quickly corrected the habit.

2. Behavior that may set a bad example for others must be addressed promptly. For example, an employee who comes to work late may lead others astray if the problem is not quickly corrected. If other employees see that one of their colleagues is getting away with wrong behavior, they may become resentful or start acting out.

3. Problems that are beginning to grow must also be handled quickly. Some issues start so small that they have

minimal effect. For example, making personal phone calls from work. If only one or two short calls are made a week, a manager may choose not to make an issue of it; but if the frequency of those calls grows to three per day for fifteen minutes apiece, the situation must be corrected.

4. Issues that have the potential to harm your business, such as leaving a door unlocked, or shipping merchandise without obtaining approval from the credit manager, must also be addressed promptly.

In the book of Judges, we see an example of a problem that required immediate action. "Everyone who saw it said, 'Such a horrible crime has not been committed in all the time since Israel left Egypt. Think about it! What are we going to do? Who's going to speak up?'" (Judges 19:30, NLT).

Some minor problems are just not worth making an issue over. Other issues are based on preferences rather than requirements, and thus should not be pursued. One manager established a policy that office workers could not eat at their desks. A more effective policy would be to allow employees to eat at their desks, but not in sight of customers and only if the food is completely cleaned up afterward. Some issues are best covered during regular performance reviews, like making a few too many personal phone calls.

5. Sometimes it can be difficult to ascertain the facts of a situation or to know for certain who might be involved. At times like these, we need to go through a fact-finding process before confronting the situation. We must also be consistent in how we treat our employees, especially when it comes to confronting them about performance issues. Scripture is clear that discrimination is wrong. If we choose to discipline one person, we must be willing to use the same standard with others, regardless of our personal likes and dislikes.

Keep a Godly Demeanor

Regardless of how we feel, we need to maintain a godly demeanor when working with employees. Losing our temper never helps. As Solomon said, "A hot tempered man...gets into all kinds of trouble" (Proverbs 29:22, LB). Staff discipline is not about us or how we feel. The purpose of discipline is to help our employees improve their performance. Likewise, cutting remarks, such as, "Since my last report, this employee has reached rock bottom and started digging," or, "This employee should go far, and the sooner he starts, the better," are counterproductive and should be avoided.

When disciplining an employee, our words must be calm, objective, and helpful. Calling someone an idiot won't help. The goal is to obtain improved performance, not to punish someone or prove that we are right. People typically don't like to be confronted, so we do well to heed Solomon's advice: "A gentle answer turns away wrath" (Proverbs 15:1). Maintaining a gentle demeanor will keep the atmosphere constructive.

If you can't keep your cool, you may need to wait until another time to discipline an employee. One time, I was told that a computer used to develop new software had crashed and that we had lost several months of new project work for a key customer. I said, "What's the big deal? Just use the backup tapes, and move on." That's when I found out that the work had not been backed up, in violation of our policy. I was so angry that all I could say was, "We'll need to take this up at another time." I knew that in my anger, anything I might say would not be helpful, and that lashing out wouldn't accomplish anything constructive. Paul writes, "Masters...give up threatening, knowing that both their Master and yours is in heaven, and there is no partiality with Him" (Ephesians 6:9). Throwing a temper tantrum or threatening is wrong in every circumstance. It is, however, appropriate to allow natural consequences to flow.

Communicate What Must Change in the Future

When we decide to confront an issue on the job, we must be clear about what must change in the future, and we must establish a timeline for these changes, so that the employee knows exactly what is expected. Solomon writes, "He who ignores discipline despises himself, but whoever heeds correction gains understanding (Proverbs 15:32, NIV). By clearly communicating our expectations, we give our employees several benefits: Not only do we help them keep their current jobs, we prepare them to earn future raises and promotions.

Be Specific
When disciplining an employee, we must:
- remain objective
- state clearly and specifically what must change and by when
- clearly define the consequences if the desired change does not occur.

Rather than say, "Your sloppy work needs to improve," be specific about the results you want to see: "We require that customer invoices have an accuracy rate of 99.5 percent, and we expect you to meet that standard. Your current accuracy rate is 97 percent. We expect you to raise your rate to 99 percent within one week and meet the 99.5 percent standard within thirty days."

Confirm the Consequences of the Situation
Explaining the consequences of a situation will help your employees understand the importance of changing. Solomon writes, "Whether a tree falls to the south or to the north, in the place where it falls, there it will lie" (Ecclesiastes 11:3, NIV). When a tree is cut down correctly, it falls in the right place, safely away from the house or your car. But whether the tree is cut correctly or not, it will fall somewhere. When we explain to our employees the consequences of incorrect work, it helps them understand the importance of doing the job right. For example, explain to your billing department how billing errors cause invoices to be returned, which hurts cash flow, creates more work, and damages the company's credibility with

customers. Employees who are being disciplined are less likely to feel picked on if they see the logic and wisdom in your correction. Help them to see the situation from the customer's perspective by asking, "How would you feel if you received incorrect invoices that had to be returned?"

Obtain Agreement that a Change Will Happen

Next, obtain agreement that the person will change in the future. Acknowledgment and agreement ensure that you have been heard and understood. Further, the commitment establishes a benchmark for further action, if needed. You want your employees to confirm that they *can* make the change, they *want* to change, and they *will* change.

An employee who says, "I'll try to be at work on time each day," is not committing to anything. Instead, what you want to hear is, "Yes, I acknowledge that being late is a problem, and I will be on time every day." Likewise, "I'll try to make a better effort to reduce invoicing errors" is not a promise; but "I will review each document for accuracy and meet the standard" is a firm promise.

State Clear Consequences if Change Does Not Occur

When we sin, we bear the consequences of our sin. On the job, the result may be a written warning, suspension, loss of future wage increases, or termination. Consequences are the normal results of our actions. Employees deserve to understand the consequences that will apply should improvement not occur. Solomon writes, "Words alone will not discipline a servant; the words may be understood, but they are not heeded" (Proverbs 29:19, NLT). "A worker's appetite works for him, for his hunger urges him on" (Proverbs 16:26). Keeping their jobs should be motivation for your staff, and we need to honestly communicate when an employee's actions are putting his or her job in jeopardy.

For example, rather than say, "If you come in late one more time, you're fired," we must clearly explain the company's policy in advance. For example, "Our policy is that more than three late arrivals in a month will result in a written warning. After two written warnings, the consequence will be a one-day suspension, followed by dismissal if late arrivals continue."

When an employee violates company policy, rather than rant about it, simply explain the problem, the necessary change to be made, and the possible consequences: "Last week there were six errors in pricing in customer invoices, resulting in bills being returned for correction. Our standard is no more than one error per week. I am asking that in the future you check and verify the correct price before the customer invoice is sent. This is the third time I have brought the same problem to your attention. If the same error occurs in the future, you will receive up to two written warnings, followed by dismissal if you are unable to meet the standard."

Discern Between Willfulness and Ignorance

Jesus taught, "That servant who knows his master's will and does not get ready or does not do what his master wants will be beaten with many blows. But the one who does not know and does things deserving punishment will be beaten with few blows" (Luke 12:47-48, NIV). We need to establish whether an offense was committed willfully or unknowingly. Treat ignorant mistakes as learning opportunities.

Ongoing Monitoring Needed

We need to follow up to make sure that promised changes happen. Peter writes, "A sow, after washing, returns to wallowing in mire" (2 Peter 2:22). If we don't follow up, our employees may revert to the same bad behavior, or they may not change at all.

Positive changes should always be reinforced as an encouragement. When we notice improvement, we should positively reinforce it. For example, "Tom, I noticed you have been on time every day for the past three weeks. Excellent improvement."

Of course, if improvement does not occur, we must address that as well. "Tom, I noticed you have been late twice this month, and I wanted to reinforce my earlier comments on the importance of being at work on time."

If you are unwilling to follow through and follow up, you are better off not to confront problems. It's better to ignore problems than to confront them and then take no action. A lack of follow-through just tells everyone you're all bark and no bite. Eventually, your employees will stop listening to you altogether.

True Repentance and Forgiveness

Jesus said, "Be on your guard! If your brother sins, rebuke him; and if he repents, forgive him (Luke 17:3). Likewise, we need to be willing to offer forgiveness after changes are made. Solomon writes, "He who conceals his transgressions will not prosper, but he who confesses and forsakes them will find compassion" (Proverbs 28:13, NASB). Solomon clearly establishes that we must confess our shortcomings *and* change. A person who apologizes one hundred times, but doesn't alter the bad behavior, has not forsaken the bad behavior. When change does occur, we need to forgive and forget past infractions, just as the Lord forgives us. However, some offenses on the job—such as dishonesty, criminal behavior, or gross negligence—may require discharge without grace.

Case Study

George sold advertising for a group of radio stations in a large city. He had been employed for eighteen months and had passed his 90-day probationary review with little comment. His annual review was considered satisfactory. His sales production totals were slightly over the minimum required.

Walter, the sales manager and George's boss, spent seventy percent of his time calling on customers, leaving little time for management responsibilities.

Over time, George developed several negative habits. First, he tended to come in after the 8:30 starting time, often considerably late. In addition, he often dressed too casually—despite the dress code, which required a coat and tie—on days when he was scheduled to remain in the office. Consequently, on three occasions he responded to urgent customer requests and made visits to customers without a coat and tie.

In addition, a sales log was required to be completed for each outside call, and George often missed the Friday deadline for turning in the log and expense reports. When a customer agreed to an advertising contract, the signed agreement was required to specify all pertinent details. Six times, George omitted some important details, requiring him to return to the customer and obtain a revised agreement. On one occasion, a twenty percent discount was offered to a customer without approval from Walter, who required approval on all discounts over fifteen percent.

At one point, when George had been on the job for about fifteen months, Walter called him into his office and said, "Your sloppy paperwork has got to stop. Pay attention, and clean up your mess. And another thing: if you keep turning in your expense reports late, I'll just throw them in the trash."

A month later, the accounting manager handed Walter an incomplete contract from George. Walter walked over to George's desk, threw the contract down, and said, "I want this corrected immediately. You have been too sloppy with these contracts. Now go out today and get this thing signed correctly. Where's your jacket and tie? It's a disgrace to have you go out looking like a slob."

This week, Walter again called George into his office. "George, I have decided to let you go. You have been too sloppy, and I'm just tired of it. This is your last week here."

Questions:

- Would you expect George to be surprised by the news? Why or why not?
- Did Walter give George an opportunity to repent?
- Could George have been coached more effectively?
- What steps could Walter have taken to manage the situation more effectively?

CHAPTER 8

Judge All Situations Fairly

Business leaders of integrity have a responsibility to judge all situations fairly, with employees, vendors, and customers. Most managers will perceive themselves as fair all the time, but we must establish policies and procedures that ensure fairness. For example, King Solomon writes, "The first to plead his case seems right, till another comes and examines him" (Proverbs 18:17). From time to time, someone will come to us with a story and want us to take some action based on that story. Our responsibility is to understand the complete situation, and then take action based on complete facts and good judgment, not based only on our first impression.

"He who speaks rashly will come to ruin" (Proverbs 13:3, NIV). If we speak rashly, we will damage our businesses and deprive others of fair and just decisions.

Judge Vendors Fairly
Early in my business career, I was given purchasing responsibility. My company had an established relationship with a business-forms printing company. We ran several thousand forms each day through our computer printers, so we were a regular customer. Dean, the salesman for the vendor, was effective in establishing a relationship with me after I

assumed the responsibility. He was a great storyteller, and I accepted regular lunch outings with him.

Then some problems developed with the quality of the forms, causing them to stick occasionally in our printers and spoiling some forms. The cost of the lost forms was minimal, but the time and effort to rework the lost documents was labor intensive and costly. I called Dean several times to discuss the problem. One time, I insisted he come to the office at 5 A.M. to watch the printing process and see the problem firsthand. Each time, however, he minimized the problem or offered us a credit, and I allowed his smooth talk to paper over the problems. I allowed what I thought was a personal friendship to become more important than the quality of the product.

Finally, I placed a trial order with another vendor. When I told Dean, he said, "How could you use someone else? After all, we're such good friends, and we've had such good lunches." In an instant, I realized I had allowed myself to be compromised—not intentionally, not for money, but compromised from treating the situation fairly. My relationship had prevented me from taking action earlier that would have resulted in receiving a better product that would have fixed an ongoing problem. My credibility within the company was also undermined, as colleagues experienced the results of the substandard forms and believed I was doing little to resolve the issue. They saw that a good lunch with Dean would smooth over the issues, while resolving nothing.

Allowing the vendor a reasonable amount of time to correct the quality problem is fine, but allowing the problem to continue was not.

All vendors should be treated with kindness and respect. Moses writes, "Never take advantage of poor and destitute laborers, whether they are fellow Israelites or foreigners living in your towns. You must pay them their wages each day before sunset because they are poor and are counting on it. If you don't, they might cry out to the Lord against you, and it would be counted against you as sin" (Deuteronomy 24:14-15, NLT).

Taking advantage of vendors is equally sinful. As buyers, we have a responsibility to work out the best price, quality, and service, but we must maintain a respectful and professional demeanor during the process. Some vendors will respond to browbeating, screaming, and coercion, but best results are achieved when they want to perform.

Vendor Communication

A key element of any vendor relationship is clear communication, starting with establishing what we need. Depending on the complexity of the transaction, many companies will develop a clear outline of their requirements, using a request for a quotation (RFQ) or a request for a proposal (RFP). If we're going out for a bid, but we give one vendor more, or less, information than the others, we are not being evenhanded, and we are guilty of discrimination. We need to be responsible to create a level playing field in the interest of fairness, and to protect our own company's best interests.

Effective vendor communication should always be two-way—we share what we need, and the vendor is given an opportunity to furnish feedback and offer creative ideas that may improve our situation. Solomon writes, "Though good advice lies deep within the heart, a person with understanding will draw it out" (Proverbs 20:5, NLT). A wise question to ask every salesperson is this: "Do you have any ideas to improve our process, our system, or to serve our needs?" Drawing out a vendor can be a great source of information and improve our understanding.

Negotiate in Good Faith

At times, companies will ask for quotations with little or no intention of using them. I have made sales proposals in circumstances where I learned that the incumbent would be keeping the business regardless of how comprehensive my service proposal was or how low the price. All the prospect was doing was gathering quotes because company policy dictated that three bids must be tendered each year. Asking for bids with no intention of treating those quotes seriously is a waste of time and money, and a show of bad faith.

Further, I believe in asking for the best price first and not disclosing bid information from one vendor to another. Often we may want to take a lower price to our incumbent vendor, whom we like, and ask them to match the price. From my view, this is using the other vendor just to get a lower price. If I want to keep my established vendor, based on overall service and value, then I pay the higher price. If price is my key factor, I make the change and advise the previous vendor that they lost the business due to price considerations.

Giving unsuccessful bidders the reason why they failed to win the business is helpful to them and may assist them in the future at crafting more effective proposals. For example, I have been told that we lost bids based on price, and that price would be the key factor in future decisions. This feedback allowed me to propose only the lowest cost options, reducing service options in return for a lower price. As a result, I won some future business by meeting the customer's stated goal of getting the lowest price.

Keep Your Part of the Deal

After reaching an agreement, we must keep our side of the bargain. Payment terms are a fair issue during negotiations, and by all means we should get the best terms we can. But once the terms have been established, we need to honor them. Some companies that have agreed to a two percent cash discount for payment within ten days will pay in fifteen to twenty days and take the two percent discount anyway, believing the vendor won't complain or thinking that the two percent discount is built into the price anyway.

The prophet Hosea writes, "They spout empty words and make covenants they don't intend to keep" (Hosea 10:4, NLT). Some businesspeople have little intention of keeping payment terms. But when we pay late, we have made an empty promise.

On the other hand, when we keep our part of the bargain, we may be able to get a better price or terms in the future. During negotiations, I have reminded vendors that my company has paid reliably and on time, and have asked if that allows them to give us a better price. On one transaction, I was a little late in having a check sent for $7,000. I called the company and apologized for failing to pay within thirty days. The vendor was surprised I had called, and said, "Payment was received in 35 days, and that's fine." Still, my call established my personal integrity with a key business partner.

Maintain a Kind Demeanor

When we have the power of giving or withholding business, we can easily become arrogant. Solomon writes, "Some people make cutting remarks" (Proverbs 12:18, NLT), and though we need to be factual, we can be kind and not cutting. The apostle Paul instructs, "Get rid of all bitterness, rage, anger, harsh words, and slander, as well as all types of evil behavior. Instead, be kind to each other, tenderhearted" (Ephesians 4:31-32, NLT). No one likes to be beaten up by a customer.

We need to be careful not to confuse direct, clear communication over issues with being unkind. Saying to a vendor, "Two percent of your last shipment failed to meet our specifications, and if future shipments do not meet our standard of quality, we will need to place the business with a different vendor," is clear, straightforward communication. Saying, "Two percent of your last shipment failed to meet our quality standards, and if you don't stop sending us junk and straighten up, we'll find someone else," is unnecessarily harsh and abusive.

Judge Customers Fairly

A company that sold used computers offered a 30-day warranty. The owner gloated that if a customer came in on the thirty-first day, too bad, nothing would be done, regardless of the circumstances. He wouldn't even look at the computer. Though a 30-day warranty may be reasonable, the owner's attitude toward his customers was telling. Clearly, even if a customer brought back a unit six months later, holding to the warranty would be reasonable. Paul writes, "Serve wholeheartedly, as if you were serving the Lord, not men" (Ephesians 6:7, NIV). We need to judge customer issues in a balanced way by asking several key questions:

- Did we do what we said we would do?
- Did the customer suffer loss?
- Did the customer take more time and trouble based on our error?
- Can we make a reasonable accommodation, even if we are not required?
- Have we made every effort to be fair?

Ezekiel writes, "Let not the buyer rejoice nor the seller mourn" (Ezekiel 7:12). When negotiating with customers, we need to keep a balanced perspective. A coin dealer who occasionally had people walk in with collections to sell from estates, typically offered ten to fifteen percent of the value, knowing that if the people shopped around he would lose the deal, but also knowing he would make a killing if his offer were accepted. We are entitled to a competitive return in the marketplace, but we should not take advantage of a person's ignorance.

Treating customers fairly does not require that we give in to every demand or request, but if we have to make an adjustment, it should fit the circumstances. If we fail to ship on time, we may need to offer to cancel the order, issue a credit adjustment, or give free expedited shipping to meet the promised deadline. However, we don't need to give away $5,000 worth of products just because we missed the shipping date. And dry cleaners who are unable to remove a stain from a pair of pants, having cautioned the customer that the effort might not be successful, are not responsible to buy a new pair of pants just because the customer has a fit. On the other hand, if the dry cleaners lose a $200 pair of slacks, they must replace the pants with similar quality, not a $15 pair.

Judge Employee Issues Fairly

Employee disputes and issues will come up every day, requiring us to make good judgments. King Jehoshaphat instructs, "Do not judge for man but for the Lord who is with you when you render judgment. Now then let the fear of the Lord be upon you; be very careful what you do, for the Lord our God will have no part in unrighteousness or partiality or the taking of a bribe" (2 Chronicles 19:6-7).

We may blame employees for making mistakes, but before we place blame we need to make sure we understand what happened and who was responsible. One time, I took a customer complaint over the phone, and pulled the file so I could call the customer back. Just then, my boss happened to walk by. He picked up the file, looked at the mess, and said, "This file is a trail of incompetence. What the ____ are you doing?" The truth was that it wasn't my issue or my mistake— I just happened to be the one who answered the phone call— but now I was getting the heat for the problem. We have probably all been on the receiving end of one of these misunderstandings. As managers and supervisors, we need to make sure we understand the true situation before we fly off the handle.

We also need to consistently enforce our policies with each employee. If we hold one person accountable for late arrivals, we need to hold others accountable as well. Additionally, we can't get involved with judging what a reasonable excuse for tardiness is and what is not. We need to ask our employees to arrange their schedules to ensure on-time arrival. When we excuse someone based on a good story or excuse, we are actually treating one late arrival differently from others.

Any punishment must fit the crime, as well as be evenhanded. It wouldn't be fair, for example, to fire an employee for the first late arrival. We need to establish standards that most people can adhere to and that are important for the business. Our standards should be based on something we have done before, can do, and are willing to do again in the future. In other words, don't discipline one employee for an infraction unless you would be willing to discipline every employee for the same infraction.

Some standards may be more demanding for one set of employees than another, such as sales targets for top pay scales. We would expect a higher level of productivity from a $200,000-a-year salesperson than for a $60,000-a-year salesperson. Our responsibility is to establish reasonable and fair standards, and then hold consistently to those standards.

Treating every employee fairly is a key to improving our businesses. We have the responsibility to hire and promote the best people, and judging employees fairly is an important part of that. Furthermore, treating everybody consistently will improve morale in your department and your company.

Finally, when we show partiality, it actually affects the very one we like. Look at the example of Jacob: "Jacob loved Joseph more than any of his other children because Joseph had been born to him in his old age. So one day Jacob had a special gift made for Joseph—a beautiful robe. But his brothers hated Joseph because their father loved him more than the rest of them. They couldn't say a kind word to him" (Genesis 37:3-4, NLT).

King Solomon instructs, "To show partiality is not good" (Proverbs 28:21). We need to ensure that we show no partiality with vendors, customers, and employees.

Case Study: The Diner

Tom and Brenda had operated a diner for twelve years. During that time, they developed a steady clientele. The restaurant had sixteen employees, both full-time and part-time. Several employees complained that Mimi received the most flexible schedule. Brenda explained that Mimi had a lot of life challenges and needed the consideration. Complaints persisted, and several waiters made the point that Mimi received the busiest times, allowing her to earn more tips than the others; but Brenda told them, "That's the way I want it."

Tom did the buying and was struggling with keeping costs down. When his produce vendor told him that prices were going up again, Tom called several other suppliers who had given him better pricing in the past, but they also quoted higher pricing. In the past, Tom had taken lower price offers back to his regular vendor to match. Now, he was facing higher prices and no good alternatives.

He called back his regular supplier to ask if the prices could be cut. The salesman said, "No, that's the best we can do. Besides, you keep taking the cash discounts even when you don't pay in ten days, and your account, which is supposed to be thirty days net, regularly goes past ninety days. Also, your reject rate is very high, and we're wondering if you just order too much, and then when stuff starts going bad, you want a credit. Frankly, my boss is wondering if he really wants your account. I was going to call you, but given all the issues, we are increasing prices eight percent starting the first of next month. If the new pricing is not agreeable, then you are free to look elsewhere.

Just then, two of the best table servers gave notice; they were going to another diner. The reason given was that they needed to be given better hours when the opportunity for tips would be higher.

Questions:
- How could the work schedule been done differently?
- Should the other staff been agreeable to the arrangements granted Mimi?
- Will the business be better or worse staffed as a result of the resignations?
- On the surface, was Tom ethical with his supplier?
- What price is he paying now as a result?

CHAPTER   9

Listen Effectively and Seek Positive and Negative Feedback

Business leaders have opinions, often strong opinions. Leaders are leaders because they develop a vision of what needs to be done, communicate that vision, and then accomplish it. A strong, clear idea of what needs to be done is great on one level, but we also need to develop the ability to hear others.

The author of Hebrews writes, "It is hard to explain, since you have become dull of hearing" (Hebrews 5:11). Every day, we will be told bits of information that we need to hear, understand, and act on if we are going to be successful.

Listen to Counsel

We have covered the need to obtain and listen to wise counsel. Solomon writes, "The way of a fool seems right to him, but a wise man listens to advice" (Proverbs 12:15, NIV). When we decide that we don't need to listen to others, we define ourselves as fools. On the other hand, we should only ask for input if we really want to hear it. Have you ever been in a restaurant and had the waiter come over and ask if everything is OK—and then turn and start walking away before you can even answer? You feel like, "Why even bother asking?" It's better not to ask than to ask and not care about the answer. But of course it's even better to ask, listen, and then act.

Invite Listening Opportunities

It takes work to invite listening opportunities. They don't just happen; it takes planning and follow-through. We need to establish a culture in our businesses of respecting the ideas and thoughts of others. Also, we need to set up an orderly process to nurture those ideas and keep them coming.

We need to develop effective listening from our peers, employees, and customers. Each group needs to be cultivated differently, but all are important to our growth and survival.

Listen to Your Customers

Customers are a great source of feedback. Some will tell us what they like; others will tell us what they don't like; and some will send a message by withholding their business. Most customers will not tell us when they are unhappy, so when we receive negative feedback, that person may represent the views of a hundred other customers.

Every businessperson must spend time with customers. General Electric requires all directors to visit several key customers each year to ensure direct feedback. Regardless of how busy you are, find a way to get direct feedback from your customers.

A restaurant owner can't spend every minute in the kitchen. Watch customers when the food is delivered. Are they delighted? What food is left on the plate? If vegetables tend to be left, is the quality and appearance up to standard? Are customers kept waiting for the check, and are the water glasses kept filled? Customers will tell you by their body language how satisfied they are.

George's discount furniture store offered great prices and selection. Everything was sold cash and carry with no delivery options. The owner made a habit of wandering the sales floor, chatting with customers, and working as part of the sales team. He noticed that a lot of older customers would come in, look around, and leave. He started up conversations with several of these people and learned that most of them needed help with delivery. Without that option, they would not buy, regardless of how great the deals were.

George didn't want to take on the burden of delivery, even with an added charge, because the time and overhead cost would adversely affect his business model. But after watching more customers depart based on the lack of delivery service, he cut a deal with an outside delivery company. Those customers who wanted a delivery service could make arrangements through that company. As a result of listening to and acting on customer feedback, George was able to maintain his business model and increase his sales.

When interacting with customers, develop the habit of asking questions: What do you think? Why do you say that? How can we do better? Is there any new product or service you would like us to offer? What's working and not working? Be careful not to become defensive when receiving customer feedback. Remember, they're doing you a favor by giving you their honest perspective. Granted, a few customers are sourpusses and will never be happy, but as you receive comments, filter them carefully to determine how you can improve your business and serve your customers better.

Here's the most important question you can ask a customer: Would you refer us to others wholeheartedly? If they say yes, you have a solid customer relationship. If you can develop a customer referral system, whether by using coupons, gathering names, or offering incentives for referrals, you can gauge how often you receive new business as a result of referrals. If you are receiving referrals, or if the number is increasing or decreasing, you can gauge how satisfied your customers are with your company.

Listen to Your Staff

As leaders, it's easy to believe that we are supposed to have all the answers, and that asking employees for input is a sign of weakness and indecision rather than an indicator of strong leadership. However, King David, whom the Bible portrays as a strong and able leader, "consulted with the captains of the thousands and the hundreds, even with every leader" (1 Chronicles 13:1). Given the size of the Israelite army at that time, David would have personally consulted with more than a thousand people. In addition, the use of the word *consulted* implies that David was actually looking for advice and feedback, not just chatting and spending idle time.

Employees can give us valuable feedback; however, we must demonstrate that we genuinely want feedback and honest communication. We may say we have an open door policy, but if we fail to listen receptively, we would be better off keeping the door shut. James writes, "Everyone must be quick to hear, slow to speak and slow to anger" (James 1:19).

When we are supposed to listen, we need to stop what we're doing, look up, and establish eye contact. People communicate with body language even more than with words, so it behooves us to watch as well as listen. Job was asked, "If one ventures a word with you, will you become impatient?" (Job 4:2). If we look impatient, we will cut off the information we need to hear.

We have all been subjected to various conversation turnoffs. The *paper shuffler*, who looks at correspondence, invoices, or other documents while you're talking. The *wandering eye*, who looks everywhere but at you. The *multi-tasker*, whose eyes are glued to the computer screen, clicking on emails while you talk. The *yes man*, who says, "Yeah, yeah, yeah, yeah," to everything. All these responses send the message that the person isn't interested in what is being said. If you are busy, or focused on something else, stop long enough to set a time to talk later, and then keep that commitment.

When you take time to listen, repeat back what you heard to ensure understanding, and ask clarifying questions such as, "Why do you think that?" or "Can you give me an example?" These follow-up questions help to establish a dialogue and rapport.

Effective listening takes work. Experts estimate that we spend 65 percent of our listening time thinking through our response rather than concentrating on what is being said. This inattention causes us to miss key points in the conversation. Sometimes, our motivation is to be clever and quick with a response, or to demonstrate our humor. But snappy comebacks serve only to focus attention back on ourselves and away from the other person, thus stifling effective communication.

When the other person is done talking, it's okay to be silent for a moment or two. Take your time before answering. King Solomon writes, "He who answers before listening—that is his folly and his shame" (Proverbs 18:13, NIV). When we start answering, or even thinking of our answer, before we have listened, we have committed folly.

Some feedback will come in the form of an angry outburst or a comment that is off the wall, irrelevant, or just plain wrong. In these cases, we need to respond kindly but clearly. King Solomon writes, "Answer a fool as his folly deserves, that he not be wise in his own eyes" (Proverbs 26:5). The key phrase here is "as he deserves," which refers to responding appropriately, not vindictively.

We should never allow disrespectful or angry outbursts directed toward us. Anger is not a communication method; it is an unacceptable way of demonstrating feelings and ideas. If someone speaks angrily to you, ask him or her to calm down and speak in a reasonable and respectful manner. We can allow people to make blunt comments, but those comments must always be considerate and respectful.

Sometimes the feedback or suggestions we receive will be unworkable or have little merit. In those instances, we should take the time to repeat back what was said, confirming that we heard and understood what was said, and then explain our own point of view. Thank the person for bringing the item to your attention, and encourage him or her to bring up other items in the future. To take items "under advisement" or to say we'll get back to someone just wastes everybody's time. Not every idea will have merit; even though we should listen receptively to feedback, we also need to know when to stop a conversation.

Seek Both Positive and Negative Feedback

Leaders of integrity must develop a clear sense of reality. A key way to accomplish that objective is to seek both positive *and* negative feedback. A chilling word picture was written by Isaiah. "They tell the prophets, 'Shut up! We don't want any more of your reports.' They say, 'Don't tell the truth. Tell us nice things. Tell us lies. Forget all this gloom. We've heard more than enough about your "Holy One of Israel." We're tired of listening to what he has to say'" (Isaiah 30:10-11, NLT).

Throughout Scripture, the Lord used people to speak the truth. In this case, Jerusalem was destroyed, and the people were carried off into captivity as a result of failing to listen. Imagine telling someone that you want to hear lies rather than the truth! But if we're not careful, we can, in effect, convey that very message to our employees, colleagues, and customers.

Because none of us has fully arrived, and we all have room for improvement, we need to hear from others. Failing to receive feedback will cause us to lose touch with reality. I had overall responsibility for the integration of a newly purchased company. I asked a member of the accounting team how the project was going. He said, "Great, no problems."

I followed up by saying, "There must be some issues and snags ..."

"Oh no, no problems—nothing to worry about," he insisted.

I asked my colleague to take a seat and said, "I understand that you want to look on the bright side and give me a positive report, but I've been around long enough to know that no accounting conversion goes off without at least a few hiccups. I want the straight skinny." He then gave me a more honest and accurate assessment of their progress, which helped me tune in to reality and take appropriate action. I could easily have heard what I wanted to hear, declared victory, and been complacent—but that would have been wrong.

Seeking feedback will help us gather the information needed to make the best decisions. The CEO of a midsize company was preparing to announce the opening of a new facility that would employ 250 workers in a small town. Their research indicated that a great workforce was available, the county would give a great tax vacation on new construction, and all the pieces seemed to fit together—almost. As the announcement was about to be made, one of the company's managers raised a new issue: A large manufacturing company was looking at the same town and would compete for the very same workers. The CEO said, "We've made our decision, and we're going forward." Unfortunately, three months later, after the company had broken ground on the new facility and construction was underway, the manufacturing company announced its plans to build. The result was a long-term struggle to recruit the necessary workers and higher operating expenses. In this case, the CEO had made up his mind and didn't want to be confused with the facts.

Ultimately, our leadership and businesses will suffer when we do not seek out the full story and pay attention to pertinent information. A long-established restaurant was well known for its grilled steaks, chicken, and ribs, having built up a reputation over the years. Over time, some customers felt that the quality was slipping a bit—that some of the barbequed food was precooked and held over. Several customers spoke to Chet, the owner, but he ignored their comments, because he knew what a great reputation he enjoyed. June, his day manager, mentioned some of the regulars had stopped coming, but Chet said they were just getting older. The wait staff began to report that customers were complaining and sending back dinners, but Chet said, "What's the big deal? A few people complain, and when they do we get 'em a new plate." After two years of decline, sales slipped to the point that Chet decided to close the restaurant, a step he could have avoided if he'd been willing to listen to others and to act on their input.

Everything Must Be Discussable

Establishing open and honest communication is challenging, and at times painful. First, everything must be discussible. If we set certain topics off limits, we will limit the useful feedback we receive.

When managing a staff, we need to ask them how we can do a better job. Allowing employees to speak openly and honestly is difficult but necessary. I have not always been the best listener. I received feedback from several colleagues that they felt I was not willing to listen. After receiving the same message from more than one source, I prayed for insight from the Lord and came to understand that my colleagues were right. Through a variety of ways, I was cutting off feedback. Though even today I still need to work at effective listening, I have made strides as a direct result of the brave feedback I received from my colleagues.

We may have pet projects that we want to go well, and our investment in the outcome can blind us to reality. I was responsible for planning and launching a new service. The project got off the ground, albeit with some bumps, and at every opportunity I would tout the success of the new effort. I was able to allocate sales help to sell the new venture, and the accounting department absorbed more work. When the sales manager voiced some concern about expending too many resources on the new service, and the accounting department started working some overtime to keep up with the extra work, I minimized their concerns. During one meeting, as I was reporting on the success and increased profits of my pet project, the CEO challenged my numbers. "Are we really making money?" he asked.

"Of course," I responded, "just look at the P&L statement."

He asked if the extra time the sales staff was allocating was included as an expense item, and what about the extra accounting overtime? How much of my time was spent on the project, and was that included in the costs? In reality, the new service was running at a $50,000 loss, rather than showing a $50,000 profit as my P&L had shown. Ultimately, the new project did very well, but only after I stopped being blind and deaf to important information; only after I stopped listening exclusively to good news and started to seek out the full story.

Mac had a family-owned-and-operated business that employed his two sons, Bill and Don, who were both in their thirties. Bill was very effective and added a lot of value to the business, but Don was less energetic. Once or twice, Bill shared his concerns about Don with his dad, but Mac refused to talk about it. At times, other employees expressed concern about Don's ethics and follow-through, but every time, Mac refused to discuss any issues regarding his sons.

Eventually, Bill resigned to take a partnership position in another firm. Mac was devastated and asked why Bill was departing. After all, he and Don would inherit the business someday. Bill told his dad, "That's the issue. I have shared with you my concerns about Don; and though I love my brother, I can't be his business partner. Don and I are not on the same page. I needed to make a decision, and I made it." Because Mac failed to discuss the sensitive subject of his son's lack of performance, the other son left the business. Ultimately, the family business was sold and no one was satisfied.

Communication Killers

We have many ways of cutting off communication. Anger is one. As Solomon writes, "Anger causes mistakes" (Proverbs 14:29, LB). Allowing ourselves to become angry will cause us to make mistakes. If someone else expresses anger toward us, we do better by not engaging. If we respond with anger when our employees make suggestions for improvement or attempt to bring us bad (but accurate) news, they will quickly learn not to take the risk of sharing honestly in the future.

If we feel attacked, we can rephrase the negative comment as an objective statement. For example, if an employee makes a general comment such as, "You don't appreciate my hard work," you can respond by saying, "Cathy, I do appreciate everything you do. Can you tell me how I have failed to express my appreciation?" The more we're able to guide the discussion objectively, the better we'll be able to create a positive environment.

If we're arrogant and act as if we know all the answers, or if we don't allow others to finish their thoughts or express themselves before we start tearing apart their ideas, they will sense our arrogance and not share honestly with us. As leaders, we need to express confidence but in a humble way.

As managers and supervisors, we can appear aloof and indifferent if we listen but fail to respond or to confirm what was said. A lack of response is interpreted as "no, I'm not interested." If you need a few moments to think about what was said, say, "I'm thinking about what you just said, and I need a minute to process your thoughts."

Retaliation is another way to shut off communication. We may politely listen, and even give lip service to feedback, but then we wait for an opportunity to strike back. In a meeting, we may start shooting down an idea or look for a good opportunity to take a verbal jab at someone. If the person reports to us, we may add extra work, speak harshly, or take out our feelings at review time.

The reality is that people will either see us as approachable or not approachable. Our leadership will flourish the more we become approachable and allow everything to be discussable.

The Reality of Open Communication

Establishing open communication may occasionally be hurtful. We can easily talk about other people, or discuss business topics, but it's a little different when the conversation is about us. Ben Franklin said, "Those things that hurt, instruct." Solomon writes, "You will say, 'How I hated discipline! If only I had not ignored all the warnings! Oh, why didn't I listen to my teachers? Why didn't I pay attention to my instructors?'" (Proverbs 5:12-13, NLT).

We want everybody to like us, and think well of us, but no leader will be appreciated by everybody all the time. The Lord said, "Woe to you when all men speak well of you, for their fathers used to treat the false prophets in the same way" (Luke 6:26). Just as not every person will accept Jesus as Lord and Savior, not everyone will like everything we do.

Effective listening helps keep our pride in check. As we listen to the truth others share with us, we cannot help but be humble.

When we demonstrate leadership by allowing others to speak the truth to us, they will be far more receptive to hearing suggestions for improvement from us. Our departments and organizations will become more transparent and effective.

A Story of Two Kings

Look at Jehoiakim, king of Judah. Jeremiah dictated God's words to a scribe, who wrote down everything and delivered the scroll to the king. But the king "cut it with a scribe's knife and threw it into the fire" (Jeremiah 36:23). Rather than respond to God's message, the king militantly refused to listen. The result was personal destruction.

Contrast Jehoiakim's response with the response of the king of Nineveh when the prophet Jonah declared that the city was about to be overthrown: "When the word reached the king of Nineveh, he arose from his throne, laid aside his robe from him, covered himself with sackcloth and sat on the ashes. He issued a proclamation and it said, 'In Nineveh by decree of the king and his nobles: Do not let man, beast, herd, or flock taste a thing. Do not let them eat or drink water'" (Jonah 3:6-7).

Both kings heard a clear message from God. One chose to listen and respond, and his people were spared; the other ignored the warning and paid the price.

Case Study: A Costly Explosion

Sue was the CEO and majority shareholder of the Ohio Fireworks Company, which manufactured sparklers, firecrackers, and major fireworks displays sold throughout the country. Sales for Fourth of July celebrations comprised sixty-five percent of the company's annual revenue, and profit margins were high—as much as sixty percent on Fourth of July orders. Increasing sales during non-peak times was a key goal. Competitive pricing was always an issue, and Sue attempted to keep expenses down.

Safety was also a major concern at Ohio Fireworks, given the volatility of the materials. The State of Ohio Safety Board had inspected the manufacturing plant four times over the past two years, issuing violation notices for different infractions on each visit. The inspector warned that future safety violations could result in fines or prosecution. The company's insurance carrier also conducted an inspection, and as a result sent a notice that coverage would be canceled unless safety improvements were made within thirty days.

Walking through the plant one day, Sue noticed some flammable material that had been left too close to a heat source, and she instructed an employee to move the material to a safer place. A week later, a supervisor mentioned that some products were stored improperly. Sue was on her way to an important meeting and told the supervisor to talk to her later. Later that day, the insurance agent stopped by to deliver the safety report, including a list of necessary changes. Sue told the agent to drop off the report and she would read it later.

Mike, the building maintenance supervisor, asked for a meeting with Sue to cover several issues. After three cancellations, the meeting was finally held. Mike explained that he was concerned about several electrical circuits that needed repair, the heating system needed attention, and the building was receiving unbalanced heat. Because some parts of the plant were cold, employees would turn up the thermostat. Those who complained of being too warm were told to open a window.

When Mike explained that the heating and electrical problems were costly and a possible safety hazard, Sue asked whether the heating system had passed the annual inspection and if the electrical system was up to code. When he replied in the affirmative, Sue responded, "Then request more maintenance funds in next year's budget, and we'll take a look at it then."

The following Monday, Sue met with Connor, the production manager; Herb, the quality control manager; and Mike to establish a plan to comply with both the insurance requirements and the state inspectors. When Mike raised the issue of the heating system, Sue cut him off, saying, "That issue was not raised during the inspections, and I told you we'd take a look at it in next year's budget." Next, Herb said he would need $15,000 to make changes in his area. Sue told him to detail the expenses, try to cut the total amount, and get back to her. He explained that he had already reviewed the options, and that $6,000 could be cut while still complying with the letter of the correction notices, but they would have to skirt several other issues, which was not recommended. Sue said, "Keep it under $10,000."

Connor said that he would take care of everything in his area. "Great," Sue responded. "That's how I like it. Everybody, just give me an update by the end of next month, which is before the inspectors are scheduled to return."

The next afternoon, as Sue was leaving to go home, Matt, a longtime employee, stopped her and said that he was concerned that some of the newly manufactured fireworks were getting warm from the heating system before being placed in long-term storage. Sue told him to let Connor know. When Matt said that he had told Connor but that nothing had changed, Sue thanked him for the information and went home.

Five weeks later, an explosion ripped through the plant, killing three workers and injuring 27 others. The fire marshal determined that the cause of the fire was a defect in the heating system, which ignited some fireworks that had been left in the production department pending transfer to the storage room. The fire was made worse by the failure to keep all flammable material properly contained, as cited in earlier inspection reports, and by two fire doors that were left open.

Questions:
- Was Sue an effective listener?
- Did she have the opportunity to learn information that could have prevented the tragedy?
- What example can you cite where Sue demonstrated a failure to listen?
- What message was communicated by:
  - The insurance company?
  - The state safety inspector?
  - The sales manager?
  - Sue?
  - Mike?
  - Matt?
  - Connor?
  - Herb?
- What message was acted on?
- If you were the county prosecutor, would you file criminal charges?

CHAPTER 10

Communicate Openly and Honestly

The purpose of communication is to achieve understanding between ourselves and others. Effective communication starts with us. We determine what we want to communicate, to whom, when, and what action we expect as a result. King Solomon observed, "Through presumption comes nothing but strife, but with those who receive counsel is wisdom" (Proverbs 13:10). Presuming that others understand what we want, think, or expect is one of the gravest, and most common, mistakes a businessperson can make.

Informational Messages

Some messages are simply for information. The first step is to be clear about when, why, and with whom you need to communicate. Determining who needs to hear key messages is important. We do not want to overwhelm people with a lot of irrelevant material, but we do need to ensure that pertinent information is passed along.

Withholding information to exercise power over others is wrong, just as sharing inappropriately is wrong. The Lord said, "No longer do I call you slaves, for the slave does not know what his master is doing; but I have called you friends, for all things I have heard from My father I have made known to you" (John 15:15). When we withhold information, we are in effect treating our staff as slaves.

The midlevel managers in a company received a memo announcing that a new computer system would be installed in three months and that their staff should not plan to take vacations during the two-week transition period. Clearly, the memo should have been shared promptly, so that the staff members could adjust their personal plans accordingly. One supervisor, however, failed to share the information with his staff. He preferred to wait and then deny requests for time off, because he enjoyed the ability to wield power over his employees. Knowledge should not be viewed as power, but as a means of enhancing the quality of the workplace for everyone.

Withholding some information—based on whether or not there is a need to know—is in the best interest of the business and the staff. Confidential competitive information should not be shared, because if it leaked out, the business would suffer harm. A simple question to ask before sharing information is, "How will the information be used, and what actions will the staff take differently as a result?"

Some information will come from the outside—from vendors, competitors, news reports, and "the word on the street." Wise leaders realize that their employees will hear more than the leaders realize, and thus they proactively give out appropriate information. For example, the owner of a large grocery store learned that the town's largest employer was closing. The owner "didn't want to scare anyone" by addressing the concern, but in reality, the employees had already heard the news through other channels; they had friends and family who would be directly affected, and they were concerned. By addressing the concern up front, including a statement that a hiring freeze would be imposed, the owner could have demonstrated to his staff that he was taking prudent action.

Employees will often fear the worst, so straight talk from management keeps everyone informed.

Instructions and Directions

We have a responsibility to be clear with our instructions, and to accept the responsibility for clarity. "Moses carefully wrote down all the Lord's instructions" (Exodus 24:4, NLT) and King Solomon, the wisest person ever to live, "taught the people knowledge" (Ecclesiastes 12:9).

Because some people learn better by hearing, and others by seeing, the best instructions are given both orally and in writing. When training, we can provide a good model by having the new employees watch us do the task—and then we watch them. In this way, we not only teach our employees, but we also learn the intricacies of the job ourselves.

When mistakes occur, we should determine whether we could have done a better job of explaining what was expected and how to accomplish the task. And we should add new ideas to our training regime. Items that are clear to us may not be clear to others. The responsibility for developing effective training falls to the managers. Written instructions serve as great reminders and are a reference for later use.

Establish consistency when enforcing company policies with staff. There is a difference between guidelines and policy. A policy is something we always do, or never do, with no exceptions. A guideline is a principle to be used on the job, while exercising good judgment.

If our policy is no cash refunds, only store credits, we cannot complain when the policy is enforced with our best customer. If we start making exceptions with our policies, those policies quickly become guidelines. Moses writes, "Do not show partiality in judging; hear both small and great alike" (Deuteronomy 1:17, NIV). When we take one person to task for violating a policy, while ignoring another's infractions, we violate the principle of impartiality. Sometimes, when our policies are poorly conceived and then backfire on us, we become angry with ourselves and take our frustrations out on our employees. Instead, we need to accept the consequences, change our policies if necessary, and not take any punitive action against our staff.

Guidelines require judgment, and thus these decisions should be delegated only to people who have demonstrated sound judgment and have received adequate training. If we have a policy, for example, to accept returns only if the merchandise is in salable condition, the judgment rests on the sales clerk to determine whether the returned item can be resold. We may want to reserve that decision for ourselves, a manager, or an experienced staff member.

Be Liberal with Praise

King Solomon understood that genuine praise is a great motivator. He writes, "Good news puts fat on the bones" (Proverbs 15:30). Every time we give a well-deserved compliment we put fat on our employees' bones.

Praise should never be disingenuous. Phony compliments can be smelled before we even speak. Praise should be given as soon as possible to gain the greatest impact. If we tie the positive feedback directly to the event, we will encourage more of the positive behavior. A great technique to practice, if possible, is to give a dinner gift certificate, a day off, or a cash bonus for an outstanding job and work effort, without waiting for a possible end-of-the-year bonus.

Some leaders withhold praise, falsely believing that people will become spoiled by hearing a positive word. In reality, withholding positive feedback is unethical; it's the same as failing to give honest feedback.

Another advantage of being generous with compliments is that our employees will then be more receptive when we make suggestions for improvement. If all they hear is the negative, and rarely the positive, they will tend to become discouraged and demoralized.

Share Positive Company News

Some business leaders want to keep financial information under wraps. But employees benefit from hearing about good results.

Moses instructs, "You shall not bear a false report" (Exodus 23:1). Failing to convey good news, with the exception of maintaining confidentiality, is the equivalent of bearing a false report. Some owners believe that if they cry poor mouth about how slow things are, their employees may be less inclined to ask for raises. In reality, our employees tend to see and to understand more than we think.

Sharing positive news is always a good motivator. We all like to be on a winning team, so why not celebrate every time we score as a team? A printing company executive celebrated every time a new account was landed. He gave his staff the credit, saying the company had won the account because of competitive pricing, and he complimented his staff for helping to keep costs down. Other times, he said that the company's fast turnaround times were the key. By sharing the positive news, and sharing the credit, he powerfully motivated his staff to keep up the good work. Sharing positive news is not only ethical, it helps to improve morale and the bottom line.

Share Negative Company News

Though it isn't fun to share negative company news, it can be just as important as sharing positive news. Moses' admonition that we "shall not bear a false report" applies to bad news as well as good.

Because sharing bad news is unpleasant, we'll be tempted to withhold it—but withholding bad news isn't helpful. On the other hand, it doesn't help to simply vent the bad news either. Leaders need to take responsibility for understanding how the bad news will affect the company and the employees, and then communicate that information responsibly. One benefit of sharing bad news with Christian employees is that it allows them to pray more specifically for the company's situation.

One company lost a large customer who represented five percent of their gross business. The CEO announced the loss of the business and implemented an immediate hiring freeze. At the same time, she assured the employees that they would not be laid off. Some people might be asked to accept a different position to help the company work through the loss of business, but they were assured of keeping a job with the company. Because the CEO was both forthcoming and reassuring, the employees were more willing to accept changes that were necessary to keep the business on track.

When an auto parts manufacturing company had its sales volume reduced by an automaker, the owner had no choice but to lay off some workers immediately. Still, he explained the slow business situation and announced the layoffs that needed to occur. Though his employees were not happy about the situation, they at least understood and respected the decision.

In the past, a small, two-person branch office that reported to me was struggling. The office was not very strategic to our overall operating plans, and they needed twenty percent more business just to break even. I spoke with the supervisor several times, using indirect phrases like, "We need more business," "You need to get out and get some business," "Business is slow," and, "We need to do better." Eighteen months later, the decision was made to close the office and offer transfers to the two employees. Both people said they were surprised by the closing and expressed dismay that they had failed to understand the situation. In retrospect, I understood that in trying to be gentle, I had failed to clearly communicate the truth.

Another location, which we had acquired through purchase, was losing money. I explained to the new staff that the office was losing a lot of money, and that was not acceptable. I told them that we would need to make some changes to become profitable. Specifically, we needed to increase business by 25 percent in one year, and reduce expenses by twenty percent to reach the break-even point. Quarterly benchmarks were shared with the employees, and our progress was tracked and celebrated. As a result, we achieved the necessary improvements and made the location profitable. Although the blunt, direct communication was difficult at the time, the result was better for the company *and* the employees.

Nehemiah understood this truth when he said, "You see the bad situation we are in, that Jerusalem is desolate and its gates burned with fire. Come, let us rebuild the wall of Jerusalem so that we will no longer be a reproach" (Nehemiah 2:17). He was blunt, but he plainly stated what needed to be done. And with God's help, the wall was rebuilt in record time.

A client told me just before Thanksgiving one year that he needed to cut twenty work positions, but he was going to hold off on the announcement until after January 1, "so as to not spoil their Christmas." I asked him, "Are you concerned about *their* Christmas, or yours? If you tell them now, they can start looking for another position while they still have a job; and though the news might be difficult to take, they may not spend as much during Christmas if they know what's coming." I emphasized that the more ethical path—though difficult—was to deal with the bad news promptly.

Provide Honest Feedback to Your Staff

We need to furnish regular and honest feedback to our employees. By establishing a policy of regular formal reviews, we commit to our employees that they will receive honest and constructive feedback at a certain time and in a particular format. Once the plan is in place, we need to be steadfast in honoring those dates. Every review done well on time is a promise kept, while every late, ignored, or sloppy review is a promise broken.

Candid feedback is best, and tough issues need to be addressed directly. Solomon writes, "In the end, people appreciate honest criticism far more than flattery" (Proverbs

28:23, NLT). The apostle Paul asks, "Have I become your enemy by telling you the truth?" (Galatians 4:16).

Feedback, in order to be useful, has to be truthful. That may seem obvious, but providing accurate feedback is not always easy. Memories tend to fade, even in just a few months, and important issues can slip away from us. We should keep a folder on each employee, into which we place notes and examples of good and not-so-good work. Keeping good records gives us two advantages. First, when we go back to the folder, it jogs our memory. Second, our notes supply us with specific examples that we can use during the review. We may have notes that document examples of great customer service or teamwork. Other notes may reveal a pattern of missing deadlines or coming to work late. The point is that by keeping good, balanced records we are able to furnish relevant, accurate, and helpful feedback.

Additionally, we need to set aside any personal biases relating to staff. Our view may become clouded based on stereotypes about the way people dress, their weight, age, physical appearance, ethnic background, mannerisms, or likeability. We need to recognize our personal filters and maintain sound professional judgment.

I allowed my judgment to become clouded by one very serious mistake that a manager made. I became harsh and quick with criticism while stingy with any praise. Finally, the manager initiated a meeting and told me I was so focused on the one mistake that I was unable to be fair. He was right, and I needed to change my thinking and perspective. Though the manager needed to be held accountable for the mistake, that accountability needed to be kept in overall perspective.

Communicate in a Balanced Way

When addressing issues candidly, we need to maintain a kind, direct, but firm demeanor. Solomon writes, "There is one who speaks rashly like the thrusts of a sword, but the tongue of the wise brings healing" (Proverbs 12:18). When we communicate, we need to use our tongues wisely, not as weapons.

Paul said, "Give up threatening" (Ephesians 6:9). We need to understand the difference between holding someone accountable and threatening them. Accountability is allowing the natural consequences of a person's actions to cause pain and discomfort. For example, sin in our lives will cause us pain and suffering. That pain is the natural result of our sin. Likewise, if a worker is lazy, unproductive, late, sloppy, or poorly suited for a job, the natural effects will be on-the-job discipline followed by dismissal.

Threatening is when we let our temper get loose and just vent our feelings. Kimberly worked as an administrative assistant for eighteen months. On balance, her work was good, but her two biggest work issues were constant late arrivals and excessive phone calls with her husband. The two problems got under her boss' skin, but he never confronted her, except to make sarcastic comments from time to time, such as, "Good afternoon," or, "Nice you could come in today," when she came in late, or, "If you're done with your personal calls, you can file these documents."

Neither issue was covered during the probationary or annual review. Finally, her boss got fed up and fired her one day. On one level, there were grounds for terminating Kimberly based on her late arrivals and the phone calls that were cutting into the work day. But was Kimberly handled with integrity? Discharging someone, other than for gross negligence or malfeasance, without addressing the issue, is unprincipled. What shape would any of us be in if the Lord did not give us warnings and give us opportunities to repent and change our ways? We need to give our employees the same opportunity.

Communicate Constructively with a Godly Demeanor

We need to frame our suggestions for improvement constructively, stating clearly what needs to change and why. When discussing dress requirements, for example, rather than saying, "You look like a slob," we should explain that customers expect and deserve a certain standard of dress. Then we should outline what we require and ask the person to comply.

We need to develop the habit of putting issues objectively rather than subjectively. Using words like *I think, I feel, sloppy, uncaring,* and *lazy* are unclear and will tend to raise the temperature of a meeting and divert the discussion down an unconstructive road. When we get into a debate about whether a person is good or bad, lazy or energetic, sharp or dull, we cross the line into a subjective argument that doesn't help. Losing our temper, yelling, or using coarse language is never helpful or acceptable, regardless of the issue. Remember, "A gentle answer turns away wrath" (Proverbs 15:1). A gentle demeanor is honoring to ourselves, our employees, and God.

It's better to be specific, using phrases such as, "Your error rate does not meet our standards," "The report you turned in is late," "The number of new customers you have brought in is below the quota for new business," or "You failed to adhere to our credit granting policy." In each case, the standard is objective, and we can confirm what happened.

Some people will be effective at skating away from accountability. Scripture asks the question, "Shall ... a talkative man be acquitted?" (Job 11:2). When we allow the discussion to become subjective, we will allow a talkative person off the hook every time. Specifics keep the debate on the issue, rather than on the person.

Intervene with Discretion

Not every little issue will warrant our intervention; we need to use good judgment. When we are unclear about a situation, we must first establish clarity before taking any action. Proverbs teaches, "Preserve sound judgment and discernment" (Proverbs 3:21, NIV).

Issues need to be confronted when:
- a situation repeats itself.
- the concern affects customers.

- when the problem will become a bad example to others.
- when the problem has a major effect on our business
- when the difficulty starts small but starts to grow.

There may be times just to let things go, such as when the consequences are minor; the issue is one of preference, not wrong behavior; or when the problem is out of character for the person. Some issues are best saved for an employee's regular, formal review.

Effective Confrontation and Communication

The first desired result of effective, direct communication is improved on-the-job performance. Solomon observes, "As iron sharpens iron, so a friend sharpens a friend" (Proverbs 27:17, NLT). We are called to sharpen the work of our staff. Our employees will learn from our example, as we see in Scripture: "Jesus went to eat dinner in the home of a leader of the Pharisees, and the people were watching him closely" (Luke 14:1, NLT). Likewise, we and our leadership will be watched closely by our employees.

Moreover, when employees heed our instruction, they will become more successful, resulting in their earning future raises and promotions. As Solomon advises, "Whoever heeds correction gains understanding" (Proverbs 15:32, NIV). When we fail to address opportunities for improvement, we stifle our employees' careers. God's discipline helps all of us grow; and though it's not always pleasant, the Lord's chastisement is key to our growth. Likewise, our discipline is important to the personal growth of our staff.

When we work to help our employees improve, we demonstrate genuine love for them. As Solomon writes, "For whom the Lord loves He reproves" (Proverbs 3:12). When we fail to communicate openly and honestly, or to intervene constructively in performance issues, we are not showing love, but contempt. True love and appreciation will give us the desire to help our staff members grow into everything that God wants in their lives.

Regarding gifts, Paul writes, " We have different gifts ... If [our] gift is ... leadership, let [us] govern diligently" (Romans 12:6, 8, NIV). We are stewards of God's property, given that the Lord owns everything. We are expected to be good stewards. When we let things slide and refuse to engage in direct communication, we cause a loss for our business that is ultimately the Lord's loss.

Follow Up for Lasting Change

When addressing issues on the job, we need to go beyond just talk. We need to share specifically what behavior must change in the future, and by when, and what consequences will apply if the person fails to make the change. We need to obtain agreement from the person that he or she is willing and able to make the necessary changes.

By obtaining an agreement that the change will be made, we have obtained a commitment that can be used to hold the person accountable. We are not guaranteed that the change will be made, but we are also not accountable for the actions of others. We are, however, accountable for our own actions. I have explained to salespeople that if they fail to meet the expected new business quota during the next three months, they will be discharged. One salesperson came in thirty percent below target, but then expressed shock and dismay when dismissed. Some people listen and respond to correction, and others simply do not.

True repentance is accompanied by a change in behavior. Solomon writes, "He who conceals his transgressions will not prosper, but he who confesses and forsakes them will find compassion" (Proverbs 28:13). Note that Solomon uses the word *forsake*, which means "to renounce and turn away from." Twenty-five confessions and apologies without a change in behavior is not true repentance.

Case Study: The Bank Officer

Brian had been employed by "The Bank" for 36 years, starting as a part-time teller at age 23, after emigrating from Europe. As a naturalized U.S. citizen, he was recruited to join the international banking department. Brian was fluent in three languages, competent in two more, and held a degree in finance from Berlin University. He obtained his master's of international finance while working for The Bank.

Throughout his career, Brian had progressed rapidly, earning regular promotions and raises while receiving sterling reviews. He was very strong in banking operations, rising to the position of international banking operations manager and then senior VP of international banking, the number two position, which he had held for eleven years.

Bob was The Bank's executive VP of international banking. Over his 37-year career, he had started the international banking department from scratch and had led the division's growth into a $7 billion international banking operation, offering letter-of-credit services, export financing, and syndication of international nation loans. Bob was creative and very strong at building customer relationships, but he was weaker in operations and detailed planning.

Brian was expert at installing the most efficient letter-of-credit system in the country, which reduced costs and added new customers. He also prepared the lion's share of the department's internal planning documents and developed effective strategies for loan syndication and use of the U.S. government's export finance system.

Brian was a little rough with some colleagues, but Bob was a master diplomat and smoothed any ruffled feathers. Bob limited Brian's involvement with staff reports when possible and rarely assigned Brian to a team, except when Brian was the leader.

Bob handled most of the key customer relationships personally and assigned banking officers to service accounts and solicit new business.

Randall was responsible for managing the growing group of banking officers. When banking officers wanted an operations person to meet with customers, Bob suggested someone other than Brian, knowing that Brian struggled with interpersonal relationships.

Each year, Bob wrote excellent reviews for Brian, ensuring that Brian received generous raises and bonuses. No mention was ever made of personal relational issues or the need to connect with customers. Porter, The Bank's CEO, was aware of Brian's shortcomings, but felt that Bob and Brian made a great pair together.

Bob announced his retirement at the same time that The Bank announced a merger with another financial institution, a deal that would result in the creation of "The New Bank." Because The Bank's international department was three times larger than the corresponding department at the other bank, Brian assumed that after eleven years as Bob's number-two man, he would be promoted to the role of executive VP at The New Bank.

As a result of the merger, every senior position was reviewed and some top positions were scheduled for elimination. When the time came to replace Bob, the decision was made to promote Randall rather than Brian. Furthermore, the top international executive at the other bank was placed in the number-two spot, and Brian was let go. He was told that The New Bank needed a leader with stronger customer relationships and better people skills.

Questions:
- Was Brian treated with integrity? Why or why not?
- What should the CEO have done?
- Could Brian have taken any steps on his own?

CHAPTER 11

Encouraging Teamwork

Teamwork is one of the most talked about and poorly executed concepts in business. When some leaders say they want to build teamwork, what they really mean is that they want to get everybody to do exactly what they say. Effective teamwork, however, will only occur when leaders:

- are willing to put team goals before individual goals
- become willing to proactively help others achieve their own goals
- value and respect their colleagues
- understand the varieties of gifts that God has given us, and value those gifts in others
- give up their need to be right all the time and
- are able to defer to a team decision when necessary.

In the book of Judges, we see an account of a major battle. A major evil was committed by the Benjaminites, and after being told about the situation, "the people rose up as one man" (Judges 20:8, NIV). Each of Israel's other eleven tribes contributed men and provisions for the upcoming battle, and then "all the men of Israel got together and united as one man against the city" (Judges 20:11, NIV). The team agreed that a sinful act had been perpetrated, and they agreed to take action together. No one was forced to join the battle; each person agreed to go.

The first day of battle went badly for the Israelites. "But the men of Israel encouraged one another and again took up their positions." Despite the defeat on day one, the team encouraged each other. After another defeat on day two, the people fasted and prayed together and received God's direction to attack the next day. Some of the Israelite army made a frontal attack to draw the Benjaminites away from the city, while others waited on the western flank to attack the city after the enemy army had been drawn away. When the Benjaminites came out to attack the Israelites on the third day, the rest of the Israelite army raced to capture the city. Then, the main army, which had been retreating, turned on the Benjaminites in a counterattack, and the enemy was completely destroyed.

Teamwork, with God's help, led to success. Likewise teamwork is a key to our future business success. We have a responsibility to become an effective part of team dynamics, whether we are the boss, a peer, or an employee.

Put Team Goals before Personal Goals

Whether we recognize it or not, an organization is a team, and the entire team either wins or loses. Losing is painful, regardless of how well we did personally. Paul understands the importance of ministry teams when he writes, "Do not merely look out for your own personal interests, but also for the interests of others" (Philippians 2:4), and "Bear one another's burdens, and thereby fulfill the law of Christ" (Galatians 6:2).

Consider a star running back, the showboat player who believes he should get the ball on every play. He may want to win, but he only does his best when the ball is in his hands. However, running backs, no matter how talented, have a responsibility to the rest of the team, and if those responsibilities are ignored, the team will suffer. The star back may be called upon to block for another runner or, during pass protection, to run pass routes as a decoy and to practice hard to assist in the development of other team members. A talented back who forsakes the team may be allowed to play at one level of competition, but the top college and professional teams will quickly discard such players. Selfish players will only reach a certain level, not because they lack talent, but because they refuse to become a part of the team. Likewise, poor team players in business limit their personal advancement and success.

As leaders, we are responsible to clearly state and communicate organizational goals. Staff members have an equal responsibility to listen to, understand, and act on those goals. Well-written job descriptions are an important part of building teamwork. Every employee needs to understand where their job fits in and how it helps the business to succeed.

Ken was a great salesman. He consistently brought in more business than any of the other eleven salespeople. A key issue for the company was that bad debt losses were affecting the bottom line. The CEO established as top priority for the upcoming year a reduction in collection times and losses. The CEO also noticed that there were problems with many of Ken's accounts. In fact, he determined that thirty percent of the credit losses came from Ken's accounts. After further review, it was learned that Ken was intentionally working to get non-creditworthy accounts approved by the credit department. For example, he would have the customer ask for a smaller credit line than needed, knowing that he would have an easier time securing a credit-line increase than he would obtaining approval for the larger credit line up front. In addition, he would not share collection concerns with the credit manager, believing that was the credit department's problem to figure out. Unfortunately, the CEO discovered that the bad debt losses exceeded the value of the new business that Ken brought in. Instead of being the star, Ken quickly became the goat.

Jack, another salesman on the staff, was more prudent. While consistently meeting or exceeding his sales quotas, he also kept an eye out for the bottom line. He was the first to inform the credit department when a new customer should be watched closely or offered limited credit. In addition, he gave the credit manager a heads-up when he noticed signs that a client was struggling. As a result of Jack's diligence, his customers represented only three percent of the company's bad debt loss. The CEO insisted that Jack's procedures become standard for the rest of the sales team.

Because Jack was willing to place the company's goals before his own, the company won, and Jack's career ultimately prospered. Ken, on the other hand, who thought he was the star salesman, but in reality was hurting the company, eventually resigned under pressure.

A good question to ask ourselves is this: Have we placed the company's goals before our own for the good of the organization?

Proactively Assist Others in Achieving Their Goals

A restaurant chain established teamwork as a key ingredient to their success. The table servers earned tips from customers, but every team member worked together to give the customers top service and a great experience. When customers were seated, the host took their drink order and gave the order to the server. Water was served promptly. When an order was ready to be taken to the table, if the server was not immediately available, another server quickly delivered the order to the table. Water glasses were continually refilled by anyone walking by, without regard to whose table it was. The result was great service and higher tips earned by all the servers. Their teamwork provided the basis for success.

Good teamwork doesn't just happen; colleagues have to make an effort to establish it. Because needs are not always apparent, we need to be on the lookout for ways to help others achieve their goals. Jesus said to the blind man, "What do you want me to do for you?" (Luke 18:41, NIV). Clearly, Jesus knew what the man wanted and needed, but he gave us the example of asking. If we just make assumptions, we may miss the mark.

One time, while working as a waiter, I was carrying too many glasses and asked someone for help. I said, "Take the red one," but the person quickly reached for another glass, thinking it was more unsteady. Unfortunately, I then dropped the other glasses, because my helper did not understand how I was holding them. We can all easily make a similar mistake, which is why asking "How can I help you?" is a good first step.

We need to take time to understand our colleagues' work and their key goals. If a key goal is to improve product quality, everyone can help. A fruit orchard owner wanted to reduce the bruising on apples. The pickers were asked to be a bit more careful. The truck drivers who brought the apples in from the orchard were asked to drive a bit slower and to avoid bumps in the road. The packers also worked more carefully, and the packing plant manager ordered different packing material that protected the fruit more effectively. When each person pitched in, the quality improved dramatically.

A department supervisor who returned hundreds of files each day for filing realized that, with a little effort, many of the files could be returned in numerical order, rather than just dumping them in a box. Two or three minutes of sorting by his employees saved a half an hour in the file room. The key was that the supervisor saw the need and reacted, even though the improvement didn't directly affect her department. Over the course of a year, the company saved 130 hours!

We need to look for problems in our areas of responsibility that affect others. In a mail room that was responsible for opening thousands of checks each day, the supervisor asked the accounting department if the process could be improved to aid in processing checks. After reviewing the process, the two managers agreed on some new procedures that saved time in the accounting department, with very little impact on the mail room.

As we demonstrate a willingness to pitch in and help others, others will be more open to helping us. As we give, we also will receive. A good question for supervisors and managers to ask subordinates during update meetings is this: Is there anything I can do to assist you in your responsibilities? Even if the answer is usually no, people like to be asked—and sometimes they'll tell you ways in which you can help.

Interact Effectively with Colleagues and Other Teams

If we become part of a workplace team, we need to make sure that we are an effective part of that team. As part of a team, we need to exchange our individual point of view for what's best for the group. Paul writes, "For the body is not one member, but many" (1 Corinthians 12:14). As Scripture instructs, no one part is of much use without the others. As a body is made up of diverse parts, so is a team.

As part of a team we need to strive to understand the entire scope of the team's projects and business needs. Paul also instructs, "Do not merely look out for your own personal interests, but also for the interests of others" (Philippians 2:4).

An auto parts store established a team a few years ago to look into a new information systems technology program for the company. During the team process, the supervisor responsible for the front-counter staff repeatedly opposed any system that would increase even slightly the amount of work for the counter staff, regardless of the benefits. Instead, we need to consider decisions from the business point of view, not our own narrow perspective.

Ultimately, a new system was selected that increased the computer input by the counter staff and the telephone order department. However, the benefits of automatic inventory control and reordering, along with the automatic generation of billing invoices, far outweighed the additional work on the front end. The key question to ask is not what each department gets out of a project, but how do we make the entire organization better?

Understand Where Your Own
Area of Responsibility Fits In

Our work affects others. Brad was speedy at order entry, completing more than one hundred transactions per day, which was sixty percent more than the average order entry clerk. Quality, however, was a problem, because Brad made an average of five errors per day, which a different department had to fix. Because Brad didn't fix his own mistakes and because his supervisor was looking only at the order entry numbers, the problem persisted. Brad even received raises because of his high productivity. If the extra work required to fix his mistakes had been factored in, however, his net productivity would have been below average, not far above average.

The prophet Isaiah writes, "So the craftsman encourages the smelter, and he who smoothes metal with the hammer encourages him who beats the anvil, saying of the soldering, 'It is good'" (Isaiah 41:7). When the smelter does a great job, the result is a better quality metal for the craftsman to work with. But a poor job smelting results in a poor result, regardless of how excellent the craftsman. Furthermore, the person doing the rough work on an anvil effectively makes the finished work much easier and saves time. In the workplace, we need to understand how the work of others affects us, so we can make suggestions for improvement.

Listen and Respect All Viewpoints
to Ensure Effective Understanding

The author of Hebrews admonishes, "Concerning him we have much to say, and it is hard to explain, since you have become dull of hearing" (Hebrews 5:11). We need to keep our minds open and respect other viewpoints to ensure understanding.

When we're part of a team meeting, we need to keep our involvement proportional. For example, on a seven-person team, we should provide about one-seventh of the input, and develop the habit of allowing others to express themselves.

Attend Team and Group Meetings Attentively

King Solomon writes, "As iron sharpens iron, so one man sharpens another (Proverbs 27:17, NIV). We need to attend team meetings to assist in sharpening others and to allow ourselves to be sharpened.

We need to be on time and not distracted. Using our Blackberrys during a meeting to check and answer messages is not only distracting to others, but it also communicates that we are uninterested in the meeting. Reading other files also causes us to lose focus. We need to keep a positive attitude. We all get tired of meetings, but firing barbs across the table doesn't help matters. If we don't like an idea, we need to avoid negative input like, "It'll never work," "That's impractical," or "It's impossible," and instead follow up with probing questions: "Why do you think that?" "How would that work?" or "Can you give me an example?" Even if we perceive something as negative, we need to keep our comments objective. For example, "This would cost our department some time, but how would other departments save even more time with this new system?"

We need to be prepared with our own completed work assignments and information before meetings, including anything needed by other team members. Paul advises, "Be diligent in these matters; give yourself wholly to them, so that everyone may see your progress" (1 Timothy 4:15, NIV). Our obvious preparation will demonstrate that we have made progress.

Being prepared highlights our leadership, even if we are not the leader of the meeting. Projects will move faster and time will be saved for others when we are prepared. Problems will surface earlier and can then be resolved faster. Involved participation also demonstrates respect for our colleagues, because it shows that we value them enough to be on time, prepared, and focused.

Ensure That Your Own Staff is
Well Informed and Cooperative

If we supervise staff or manage a department, we often need to report the results of meetings. Our colleagues and staff are depending on us for clear communication. We may be part of obtaining information or feedback for a project. Or we may need to share other information with the team. For example, a sales manager who is part of a product development team will want to keep the sales force apprised of upcoming products, so they can get a running start when the products are launched. Everyone likes to be kept up to speed. Furthermore, changes won't come as a surprise and we can solicit ideas from our staff that may be useful to bring back to our team meetings.

Know When to Back Off from Your Own Positions

When working with a team, each member needs to understand when to back off from his or her ideas, and when to press ahead. In the book of Judges, we are repeatedly told that "every man did what was right in his own eyes." We need to do what is right in the eyes of the company, not our own. The needs of others may outweigh our own.

Also, Paul said to "avoid foolish controversies" (Titus 3:9). Not everything is worth fighting for. Some issues are preferences, rather than needs. Pushing for our preferences all the time is divisive and wastes time.

We don't need to "win" every time. Besides, if we give ground on lesser issues, we'll be seen as cooperative and may actually gain more leverage for the larger issues that do matter to us. Everybody wants to feel as if they've won on at least some points.

Treat All People with Respect and Dignity

Treating every colleague with respect and dignity is a key step in establishing our integrity. James writes, "My brothers, as believers in our glorious Lord Jesus Christ, don't show favoritism" (James 2:1, NIV).

First, we must demonstrate a listening ear. Jesus said, "Take care what you listen to. By your standard of measure it will be measured to you" (Mark 4:24). As we are willing to show respect by listening to others, others will be willing to listen to us. Listening effectively is one of the best ways to demonstrate respect. We must strive to understand others before we insist that others understand us.

Take Time to Understand Diversity

Most workplaces contain different and diverse people. We need to take the time to understand these differences. Paul writes, "Esteem them very highly in love because of their work. Live in peace with one another" (1 Thessalonians 5:13, NASB).

Some differences are cultural. One person addressed ladies as "Miss Mary" or Miss Sue," a custom that came from a Southern upbringing. Offering a left hand handshake to some is an insult. Some cultures greet with a hug, some never discuss personal matters, whereas others get very personal. Our job is to endeavor to understand and work with diverse cultures in the workplace. A new arrival from England heard the music to "My Country 'Tis of Thee" playing and expressed surprise that "God Save the Queen," the British national anthem, was being played in America. His coworkers greeted this comment with hysterical laughter. We won't be sensitive to every difference, but we need to make the effort to understand other cultures and other people.

Understanding differences allows us to become more effective managers. We are all products of the culture in which we were raised. For example, a person who grew up being abused may have difficulty trusting management authority.

Ethnic diversity is another workplace reality that we need to accept and understand. Most traditional Japanese, for example, believe that talking about personal things, or using a person's first name is very rude, even after being acquainted for several years.

A friend hired some of the "Lost Boys from the Sudan," persecuted Christians who had fled the Sudan. He took them to a park, and at first they were afraid to walk in. My friend asked why, and one of the young men asked, "Is there anything in here that would eat me?" While these young men were walking to freedom, several had been attacked and killed. Their background affected everything.

Many years ago, I tossed some change on the counter at a store and two coins fell to the floor. The African-American clerk seemed to shudder. I stopped to pick up the coins and apologized for dropping them, but I said that I didn't understand the clerk's reaction. After a moment, he shared that after the passage of the Civil Rights Act, he would go into stores where the owner did not want to serve him, and they would routinely throw the money on the floor out of contempt. My dropping some change on the floor created a flashback.

Christians and non-Christians will be employed in the workplace, and we need to ensure that each is treated fairly and without discrimination.

Take Time with People in Your Organization

According to a reported story, after General Motors bought EDS Corporation from Ross Perot, Roger Smith, the chairman of GM, was in Dallas visiting EDS headquarters. When lunchtime came, Ross Perot said, "Let's go eat." Roger Smith was dismayed when, instead of entering an executive dining room, they walked into the employee cafeteria and got in line. After the meal, Smith commented that the food was pretty good. Perot replied, "The food in your cafeteria would be good too if you ate there." Perot understood that taking time to associate with his employees put him in touch with his organization.

Paul writes, "Do not be haughty in mind, but associate with the lowly. Do not be wise in your own estimation" (Romans

12:16). We need to take time to get to know people and practice management by wandering around. Having the owner or top managers demonstrate interest is a great motivator for many people. One of the best practices I started was a monthly breakfast with headquarters staff, based on the month of their birthdays. When traveling to other offices, I tried to do a staff pizza lunch or bagel breakfast. Each meeting was a treasure trove of information for me.

Reward Good Teamwork

Paul said, "For whatever a man sows, this he will also reap" (Galatians 6:7). We will build good teamwork only when we recognize and reward good team players. During performance reviews, talk about examples of good teamwork, or share examples of how teamwork can be improved. If we only talk about teamwork, while rewarding only personal performance, then we should not be surprised when our organizations fail to become great teams.

Case Study: Prairie Bakery

Prairie Bakery, a $200 million business located in Indianapolis, was installing a new computer system. Paul, the CEO, wasn't very enthusiastic about the new project—especially the time and expense involved—but he knew that something needed to be done. He appointed an ad hoc project committee (with himself as chairman) that included Elaine (Prairie's CFO), Garrett (VP sales and marketing), Leslie (VP baking operations), Tom (IS director), Richard (VP non-baking operations), and Sandra (personnel manager).

At the first meeting, Paul explained that the purpose of the committee was to assess possible software vendors, evaluate those vendors, and then select a system to take Prairie Bakery into the future. "Although I will chair the group, Tom, as our

IS Director, will lead most of the meetings and do a lot of the legwork. And I know we'll all pitch in and do our part."

Tom passed out packages from four software providers—each between 37 and 95 pages long—and explained that they should be read prior to the next scheduled meeting in three weeks. He also instructed the committee members to bring questions and be prepared to discuss how each software option would affect their parts of the company. Tom concluded by saying how excited he was that the bakery was taking this giant step into the future.

At the next meeting, Paul explained that he had not yet read the proposals, because he wanted to hear first from the operations people. Garrett was disgusted that none of the packages had a sales module. Richard brought seven pages of notes and was prepared to raise many questions about how the plans would interact with each department. Elaine had focused mostly on the cost of each plan and had skipped reading most of the detail. Leslie was frustrated that the various software options integrated most of the company but did little for baking operations. Sandra was confused about why she was on the committee at all.

When Paul asked Tom to solicit feedback about the proposals, Richard started peppering the IS director with questions, raising many issues for Tom to obtain further information. Garrett complained that because the systems failed to address sales issues, they were merely production and accounting packages. He asked to be excused from future meetings. Elaine shared that only the lower-cost plans should be considered, based on budget considerations. When Leslie handed out a baking software package she had seen at a trade show, asking that these items be integrated into the overall solution, Tom exploded. "This is an entirely different platform from anything we are considering!" Sandra remained silent.

Paul then took charge of the meeting. "Well, we have our assignments. Tom, please look into Richard's questions and get together with Leslie to discuss her perspective. Garrett, you're right; this isn't a sales package. So you don't need to stay on the committee. You can spend the time getting more business."

Nine months later, an $11 million dollar system was installed. Richard was pretty happy with the package, but immediately there were problems. Garrett fumed that special orders were not segregated from regular orders, making it difficult to track special orders from his customers. The changes needed to integrate the baking module cost $1.5 million more than planned, which frustrated Elaine. Because employees were unfamiliar with the new system, errors increased, pushing up costs and reducing customer service.

Within three months of installation, sales were down five percent. Tom was fired and Sandra resigned, tired of dealing with all the HR problems created by the failing system. The share price of the company's stock had dropped by forty percent, and annual bonuses were canceled for the staff. A week later, Paul announced his early retirement.

Questions:
- Who demonstrated the best team perspective?
- How could Paul have set up the first meeting more effectively?
- Did each person have a major stake in the outcome?
- What should have been Sandra's role on the team?
- How would you have set up the team project differently? Start with a needs analysis and explain the role of each person on the committee.

CHAPTER 12

Accommodate New Ideas

In today's changing business climate, we need to be nimble and willing to change with the times. A quick look into the past shows the peril of failing to make timely changes. Consider the transportation business. The *Quarterly Review*, a very influential publication in 1825 wrote, "What can be more absurd than the prospect held out that locomotives could travel twice as fast as stagecoaches." In 1889, the *Literary Digest* said, "The ordinary horseless carriage is at present a luxury for the wealthy; and although its price will probably fall in the near future, it will never, of course, come into as common use as the bicycle."

The buggy makers went largely out of business. However, many learned to change direction and started manufacturing parts for those new fangled cars or other new inventions that flooded the marketplace. Those who steadfastly refused to see and understand the new emergence of reality were doomed to failure.

King Solomon writes, "A wise man has great power, and a man of knowledge increases strength" (Proverbs 24:5, NIV). We can easily look back at the buggy makers and laugh, and smugly think we are different, but in reality, many of today's business leaders make equally wrong strategic decisions.

Strive for Continuous Improvement

We can choose to look at our businesses from one of two perspectives: (1) If it ain't broke, why change anything? or (2) If it ain't broke, how can we make it better? A tire maker would never recreate the wheel, but he will also never stop refining the tire! Given that none of us has personally arrived at perfection, our businesses haven't reached perfection either.

Jesus said, "He prunes the branches that do bear fruit so they will produce even more" (John 15:2, NLT). A fruit tree may produce a great amount of fruit, but the orchard manager knows that if the tree is left without care, the next crop will be smaller. Each year, branches need to be thinned to ensure that sunlight reaches all the branches. Failure to improve the tree when the harvest is great will reduce future yields. Likewise, we need to look for ways to continually improve our businesses.

If someone were to ask, "Is everything perfect with your product or service?" could we honestly say yes? Regardless of how well something works, improvement is always possible.

Most innovation comes not from a single stroke that changes the landscape, but rather from a series of innovations that bring gradual improvement. Consider the lightbulb invented by Thomas Edison. Though he created the first incandescent light, look at the thousands of changes that have been made over the years. Spotlights, different colors, bug lights, different wattages, clear, frosted, outside, Christmas lights, and night lights, just to name a few. Likewise, in any business, small steps of improvement bring tremendous changes.

One reason to improve is the reality that markets and customers will pass us by if we don't. Consider Dunkin' Donuts. In the past, they held a large market share as the go-to place for a quick cup of coffee and a box of doughnuts. When competitors such as Starbucks entered the market with upscale coffees and lattes, Dunkin' Donuts was slow to respond, resulting in a large loss of market share. At the same time, bagel shops and other doughnut shops, such as Krispy Kreme, cut into doughnut sales. Convenience stores gave customers other options for a quick cup of coffee and a pastry in the morning. Dunkin' Donuts made the mistake of believing their market position was secure. No market position is permanently secure.

Today, Dunkin' Doughnuts has taken the steps of expanding stores, realizing they need to be better positioned against Starbucks and McDonald's. Interestingly, coffee now accounts for sixty percent of Dunkin' Doughnuts sales! If the change had been understood, and acted upon in the past, they would not need to play catch up now.

The auto assembly line was first used by Ford Motor Company nearly a century ago. Today, that invention has been adopted by thousands of industries, and has been refined and customized by many companies.

Take time to review every process and product in your business. Determine what can be improved, how, and by when. If we believe we don't have time to review our products and processes, we have in fact made a decision to do nothing—a choice that may destroy our business in the future. Deciding that a business cannot be improved is like saying we cannot be improved as individuals. But I think we all would agree that we can improve as people.

Encourage New and Innovative Ideas from Others

No one has a monopoly on good ideas. Therefore, we need to cultivate and encourage ideas from others. King Solomon writes, "Intelligent people are always open to new ideas. In fact, they look for them" (Proverbs 18:15, NLT). Even King Solomon, the wisest person ever to live, understood that he needed to gain wisdom, insight, and innovation from other people.

The first step is to ask for input from staff. Many people are reluctant to share their thoughts unless asked. Develop the habit of asking for suggestions, more efficient ways to serve your customers, or new product ideas. Consider developing a formal employee suggestion program. One key motivator is publicly praising a person when we use his or her idea. Paul instructs, "Nor do we boast and claim credit for the work someone else has done" (2 Corinthians 10:15, NLT). Stealing ideas, or the credit for ideas, is both wrong and a sure way to stop the flow of ideas in the future.

When suggestions are made, we must listen respectfully and make sure we understand what is being communicated. Some employees are more articulate than others, so we should get in the habit of asking follow-up questions to draw out the answers we need, such as: "Why do you say that?"; "How would that work?"; "How would that improve customer service?" Also, we need to give employees who make suggestions feedback on their ideas, even if the ideas are not used. If possible, we should explain why we can't use the idea, thank them for making the suggestion, and encourage them to make more suggestions in the future. You never know when the next inspiration may be a big winner.

Be Aware of What Your Competitors Are Doing

Though our primary focus must be on our own business operations, we cannot ignore the competition. The prophet Obadiah writes, "You have been deceived by your own pride because you live in a rock fortress and make your home high in the mountains. 'Who can ever reach us way up here?' you ask boastfully" (Obadiah 1:3, NLT).

Sam Walton, the founder of Wal-Mart, was famous for walking into competitors' stores and taking notes. He made sure that he and his team knew what other retailers were doing. When he saw a better idea, he grabbed it quickly and implemented it at Wal-Mart.

Seigle's, a retail building products firm based in Elgin, Illinois, was supplying do-it-yourselfers long before Home Depot came on the scene. The owners visited one of the first Home Depot stores in Texas and started to cry, knowing they could not compete directly against this business model. Rather than surrender or just keep doing the same thing against very tough competition, Seigle's shifted focus to become a key supplier to building contractors and tradesmen based on the outstanding reputation they had already built for their business. They began to manufacture kitchen cabinets, doors, and windows in response to being squeezed as middlemen. The result was a great business that withstood the challenge of Home Depot and Lowe's. Had Seigle's management been ignorant of the emerging new competition, they would have been slow to react and may have even gone out of business when the big chains came to town.

Stay Close to Your Customers and Look for New Ideas

Customers are a great source of ideas. The 3M Company, a well-known leader in innovation, receives most ideas from its customers, not from in-house labs. King Solomon writes, "The fastest runner doesn't always win the race, and the strongest warrior doesn't always win the battle" (Ecclesiastes 9:11, NLT). Our strength, skills, and power in the marketplace are not enough to win. We need to get close to our customers—and stay close—to achieve lasting success.

Being Customer Driven

Many business leaders talk about being "customer driven," but what they really mean is driving their customers toward the plan they have already implemented. A true customer-driven business understands the needs, wants, and preferences of its customers, and then responds to those needs.

For example, Quicken came out with a great piece of software designed to assist people who were five to ten years from retirement in planning their financial future. Quicken was right in assessing the need for this product. People consistently fail to properly plan for retirement. Unfortunately, though the product met a need and was well priced, customers failed to buy it. Quicken's customers simply were not demanding the product. If Quicken had gotten inside the minds of their target customers, they could have learned that the demand was not there, and they could have saved tens of millions of dollars.

How well do you understand your current customers? Consider a high quality restaurant. Some customers prefer to be allowed to converse quietly and not be interrupted with nonstop "service." If the wait staff constantly interrupts customers, rather than quietly waiting at the side to be summoned, they are not customer driven. The waiters have a responsibility to size up their customers and determine how and when to offer service and when to back off. I avoid some places because they "overservice" their tables and disrupt my ability to eat in peace.

What are your customers' future needs? Customers are not forever; we need to understand not only today's needs, but their future needs as well. Look at the rapidly changing way that people use cell phones. At first, everyone just bought a phone and hoped they could get a good signal. Today, we use phones as email terminals, picture generators and receivers, Internet surfing devices, schedule keepers, and instant message machines. Cell phone companies need to understand not only how their customers use phones today, but how they will want to use them in the future.

Being Market Driven

Understanding our customers and responding is step one, but we need to go further and become market driven. We must realize that not everyone is a customer. Even Wal-Mart, the largest retailer in the United States, with a huge fourteen percent share of the retail market, has to come to grips with the fact that 86 percent of the population still shops elsewhere. Wal-Mart is constantly trying to figure out how to grab even more of the market. Wal-Mart operates one of the largest online stores, a position they reached because they realized they were gaining none of this emerging market in the past. If they had ignored this market, they would have awakened one morning in the future as a weakened company.

146

We need to understand the marketplace and the customers who are not our customers. Given our company's mission and strengths, we need to focus our efforts on the customers we are well suited to serve. The old-line department stores fell into the trap of only focusing on the customers they already had. They sliced, diced, and analyzed customer information thoroughly. Unfortunately, the change in retailing came from the discount stores. The old-line retail establishments failed to pick up on the discount trend led by Wal-Mart, Target, and K-mart. They are still paying a price today.

Most innovations will show up in the marketplace first with your noncustomers. Think about the growth of satellite TV and the competition with cable television. In the past, satellite use was found mostly among customers who had no cable options or who lived in rural locations. Cable was able to snap up customers where they were granted accesses, generally under monopoly conditions. Over time, satellite created smaller, more reliable dishes with many new innovative service options and began to directly challenge the cable companies for customers. The cable operators, who were focused on their own customer base, missed the change and were slow to react. Now, cable companies are locked in a competitive battle with the satellite TV providers.

Desert Pacific Printing in Tucson, Arizona, was a typical small print shop with a steady flow of customers. In the early 1990s, the owner began to receive inquiries from noncustomers wanting to know if they could print forms directly from a computer disk. At first, the work required tweaking the data, but Desert Pacific was able to print the jobs, thereby gaining new customers. By responding to the new trend, Desert Pacific was able to obtain new customers and hold on to existing customers. Today, nearly all print jobs are created from computer data, and printers who failed to adapt have become extinct.

When we look at the overall market, instead of looking only at our customer base, we may find that many new business

147

opportunities are available. Think about McDonald's. Even while selling billions of french fries and hamburgers, they have become the largest provider of salads in the world. McDonald's understood that there was a large market of health-conscious non-McDonald's customers who might respond to a different type of food offering. McDonald's successfully positioned itself as a supplier to this new market while at the same time holding on to its core market of customers wanting burgers and fries.

Grocery stores looking to increase sales have created grab-and-run prepared meals to compete with the fast food companies. The grocers realized that more food was being purchased in restaurants—especially fast food restaurants—and they understood that they needed to provide new, creative options to their customers.

Being Future Driven

Given that we are stewards in our businesses, we need to consider the future in everything we do. Jeremiah wrote, regarding Jerusalem, "She did not consider her future. Her fall was astounding" (Lamentations 1:9, NIV). Though the prophet was referring to the spiritual condition of Jerusalem, the same principle applies to business leaders who fail to consider the future of their businesses.

We need to stay current in our fields. Reading trade, technical, and other business magazines is one step. Another is to attend trade shows. We need to take whatever steps are necessary to understand the changing environment in our industries. Technology enhancements are affecting every business, directly or indirectly, so we need to stay current, even if we are technologically challenged.

Though occasionally a major event may herald an overnight change, most changes—even when radical—happen over time. Reflect on the temporary overthrow of King David by his son Absalom (see 2 Samuel 15:2-14). In one day, King David was routed and sent fleeing for his life. A casual observer might ask, "What happened that in one day this powerful king was put to flight?" Scripture tells us that Absalom had been working for a very long time turning the hearts of the people against his father. Though the temporary overthrow came quickly, the underlying events occurred over time.

Given the unpredictability of the future, we need to focus on changes in society and react to those changes. We need to look beyond our business models to see what is changing in the marketplace, and then react to those changes if we want to grow in the future.

Accept and Enthusiastically
Adapt to Better Ideas and Strategies

Successful business leaders have reached their level of success by being right on most things, most of the time. When we achieve a level of success, we can easily shut out other ideas, even better ideas. King Solomon writes, "When pride comes, then comes dishonor, but with the humble is wisdom" (Proverbs 11:2). If and when we allow our pride to keep us from adopting better ideas, we are poor stewards of our businesses.

When a new idea is brought forth, we should ask: "What are we trying to accomplish," and, "Will the new idea bring us closer to that goal?" We need to keep an objective viewpoint. If we start resisting a new idea, we should ask ourselves if we're just being lazy or perhaps prideful. Are we demanding to be in control, or are we reluctant because it's not our own idea?

I can give you a personal example of not listening to a better strategy. My business had a business model of extending credit liberally. Higher risk customers were granted credit, but at higher fees. Though some failed to pay, creating bad debt losses, the plan had worked well over ten years. When the economy started to turn and interest rates were rising, several colleagues cautioned that we should reevaluate our policy. I was resistant, looking back at the successes of the past several years. Even when the evidence began to mount of increased bad debt exposure, I ignored the advice. The result was several hundred thousand dollars of bad debt write-offs that could have been—and should have been—avoided.

Because we live in a time of rapid change, we need to be willing to embrace new and better ideas. The military gives us a good example. In times of war, every activity is monitored constantly for results. Different tactics are tried and evaluated, and the most successful are implemented quickly because lives are at stake. When the enemy changes tactics, the changes are analyzed and new countermeasures are developed. Likewise, in business, we need to be constantly reevaluating our strategies and tactics and adapting to today's marketplace.

When presented with a new proposal, ask yourself, "What is the cost of implementing this new idea, and will that cost be worthwhile?" Also, "What is the cost of not changing?" In principle, more new initiatives will fail than will succeed. No one likes to fail, but the key principle is that we need to try more than one idea and be willing to discard those that don't work well.

Treat Mistakes as Learning Opportunities

In the past, a key researcher at General Electric made an error that cost the company more than $20 million. The researcher resigned, feeling responsible for the failure. The CEO called the researcher and asked him to stay. "After all," he said, "we just spent $20 million training you." The researcher stayed and led many future successful projects. As businesspeople, we may have ten year's experience, or one year of experience ten times. The difference is what we have learned from each mistake or "learning opportunity." Solomon writes, "Better a poor but wise youth than an old but foolish king who no longer knows how to take warning" (Ecclesiastes 4:13, NIV). Each mistake is a warning that we need to change direction. Our choice is to heed each warning, or not.

We need to establish our objectivity in every instance. We need to contemplate the following key questions: What went wrong? Why did it go wrong? What will fix the problem? Any defensiveness on our part will only short-circuit the process. When we confess our errors, others will feel safer in admitting their own errors or miscalculations, thus creating a stronger company culture for improvement in the future.

Herb ran a local bakery very successfully, then he opened another store across town. Unfortunately, though Herb was a great baker, he was a poor manager. The new location was poorly run and lost money from the start, with little sign of improvement. Rather than admit that the idea wasn't working, Herb focused more time and energy on the new store, but without results. When Herb was advised to hire an effective manager, he ignored the suggestion. Rather than close the new store and cut his losses, he persisted. The eventual result was the bankruptcy of his entire business.

One of my favorite interview questions to ask is this: "Tell me about your three biggest mistakes and what you learned from them." Some job candidates who lack candor are reluctant to share. Others disclose several examples and demonstrate that they have learned each lesson well. These folks go to the top of the prospect list.

When we confess our errors, mistakes, and miscalculations to others, they will have more confidence in our leadership in the future. Would you want to follow a leader who continues to make the same mistakes and judgment errors? Colleagues will develop more, not less, confidence in our leadership when we learn and grow with each mistake. Confession and an understanding of what needs to change allow us to improve in the future.

Case Study: Stubborn Management

World Auto Repair was a national chain of auto repair garages with 235 locations, mostly in the Midwest. Dennis was the Southwest operations manager, overseeing 27 locations in West Texas, New Mexico, and Arizona. He reported to Bill, the

VP of branch locations, and was responsible for overall profitability, cost control, local sales and promotion, inventory management, and hiring garage managers.

The company typically earned a margin of eleven percent nationally on sales, but historically the margin in the Southwest region was nine percent. Bill met with Dennis in January and told him that margins in the Southwest region needed to improve by two percent by the end of the year. Dennis was annoyed and told Bill that things were different in the Southwest compared to other regions of the country. "Besides," he said, "the division is making money." Bill explained that each facility was expected to improve its margins each year, and Dennis needed to develop a plan within thirty days for his approval. A follow-up meeting was scheduled for six weeks later.

Two weeks later, Dennis held a retreat for the garage managers in the region. Key suggestions for improvement included the following:

- Spend more on advertising.
- Give more "specials" as an incentive to win new customers, and then sell them more work.
- Raise prices by seven percent (two percent more than expected cost increases) to obtain the needed margins.
- Improve inventory control to save on inventory expenses.
- Start advertising in Spanish, and hire bilingual staff to appeal to the growing Spanish-speaking population.
- Close three garages that were declining in sales and in areas that were declining economically. One was losing two percent, another was earning only three percent, and the other was earning four percent.
- Ask that the corporate overhead allocation be reduced.

At the follow-up meeting, Bill refused to listen to the idea of developing a Spanish marketing plan. "We just market effectively to everybody," he said. When Dennis tried to explain that the market in the Southwest was different, Bill said, "No.

One country, one marketing campaign." Bill also torpedoed the idea of closing any outlets, saying, "We never close anything, we just go forward. Just make 'em work." Dennis then suggested raising prices slightly at the unprofitable locations to cover the higher operating costs. Bill said that pricing was determined on a national basis and would not change.

Dennis admitted that he had not done a satisfactory job of keeping parts inventories at the right levels, but he was already taking action to adjust inventories, which would save $60,000 a year.

Dennis was authorized to increase the marketing budget but would be held accountable for the results. He wanted to change some of the advertising to appeal to the regional clientele, but Bill said no. All TV, radio, and newspaper advertising was developed by the marketing experts at the corporate office.

Questions:
- What counsel would you give Bill?
- What counsel would you give Dennis?
- What are Dennis' prospects for achieving the required target?
- Which ideas did Dennis seem to embrace and which did he not embrace?
- Who seemed more defensive?

Paying Taxes

Few of us enjoy paying taxes. Given a choice, we would all pay less. Even when political leaders denounce tax cuts at the federal or state level, or are disappointed when a tax increase fails, you never see these folks voluntarily paying more taxes. Let's face it, if we really wanted to pay more taxes, we could just go ahead and pay extra.

In 2001, Governor Mike Huckabee of Arkansas refused to raise taxes and instead established a "Tax Me More Fund," through which the citizens of Arkansas could contribute directly to the state's general fund. The governor challenged all the pundits who were saying that state residents wouldn't mind an increase or who said they would pay more if given the opportunity. He gave them the opportunity. According to press reports, a total of $1,000 was contributed to the fund, thus confirming what we already know: we don't like to pay taxes.

Does the Bible Support Paying Taxes?

When John the Baptist was admonishing sinners and baptizing people in the wilderness, "some tax collectors also came to be baptized, and they said to him, 'Teacher, what shall we do?' And he said to them, 'Collect no more than what you have been ordered to'" (Luke 3:12). When John told these people to stop sinning, it was clear that extorting more taxes than were due was sinful and must be stopped; but he never said the tax itself was not valid. John was not shy when pointing out sin, and I believe he would have said, "Stop collecting taxes" if the tax system itself were sinful.

The scribes and the chief priests asked Jesus, "Is it lawful for us to pay taxes to Caesar, or not?" (Luke 20:22). Jesus responded, "Render to Caesar the things that are Caesar's, and to God the things that are God's" (v. 25). If Jesus had intended to say that taxes were not lawful, he would have taken this opportunity to say so. Instead, he endorsed the idea of rendering to the government what belongs to the government.

Another instance of tax-paying in Scripture relates to the Temple tax. This was not a government tax, but it was part of the Temple worship system. Peter was asked, "'Doesn't your teacher pay the temple tax?' 'Yes, he does,' he replied" (Matthew 17:24-25, NIV). Later, the Lord said to Peter, "So that we may not offend them, go to the lake and throw out your line. Take the first fish you catch; open its mouth and you will find a four-drachma coin. Take it and give it to them for my tax and yours.'" (Matthew 17:27, NIV). Earlier, the Lord had explained that he was not required to pay the tax, but as Scripture indicates, he paid the tax anyway to avoid offending. Given that the Lord did not sin, paying the tax was not a sin.

In the Old Testament, when Israel was clamoring for a king, the prophet Samuel explained the cost of rulership. "He will take the best of your fields and your vineyards and your olive groves" (1 Samuel 8:14). Further, Samuel said, "He will take a tenth of your seed and of your vineyards" (1 Samuel 8:15), and "He will take a tenth of your flocks" (1 Samuel 8:17). Samuel was clear that a tax system was part of the price of being governed.

The apostle Paul writes, "Render to all what is due them: tax to whom tax is due" (Romans 13:7). Based on these scriptural examples that do not condemn taxation as wrong—

only the unfair extortion of more tax than is owed—I believe we must pay taxes, regardless of how much we may dislike them or believe the tax code is unfair.

Honesty in Filing

If we're going to pay taxes, we need to be honest. Anytime we sign a tax document, either as an individual or for a business, we are giving our word. James writes, "Above all, my brothers, do not swear—not by heaven or by earth, or by anything else. Let your 'Yes' be yes and your 'No,' no, or you will be condemned" (James 5:12, NIV).

Any statement we make, every document we sign, must be accurate. Whenever we sign a tax document that we know is false, we violate the Scriptural command to be truthful in everything we say. Our yes to the question of how much money we made is not to be "mostly yes," but should confirm the exact amount.

Paul writes, "Everything is pure to those whose hearts are pure. But nothing is pure to those who are corrupt ... because their minds and consciences are corrupted" (Titus 1:15, NLT). In business, as with any other part of our lives, we have a choice to either become people of integrity or not. Despite whatever temptations we face, we still have a choice. The answer is either yes, we are people of integrity in every aspect of our lives, or no, we are not. Yes, we have all sinned and fallen short of God's glory; but when we sin, we are told to confess that sin, repent from that sin, and stop doing that sin. False tax returns are a sin from which we can and must repent.

A client called me one day for advice on buying an ice cream stand in a resort area. He owned a cottage in the area and thought the business might be good for his kids to have a part in running. The seller showed a profit of $15,000 a year on his tax returns, but he told my client that he really made $80,000 a year but didn't report the true balance on his return. I said, "Well, we know for a fact this man is a liar. He has either lied to the government or he is lying to you now about how much money he's made. Either way, I would not trust anything he says." My client passed on the business, and I later learned that the store sold for much less than an $80,000 bottom line would dictate. Apparently, whatever money the owner had saved by not paying the proper taxes, he lost (and possibly more) when he sold the business.

Another client, Wally, called me and wanted to open a Nevada corporation to save taxes, even though all his business was conducted (and would continue to be conducted) in Arizona. I explained that under the Arizona tax code, all business done in the state must be taxed under Arizona law.

Wally said, "How will they know? Why can't I just act as if I now live in Nevada?"

I explained that if he were caught, fines, penalties, and possible criminal charges could be levied. "More importantly," I said, "the Lord knows what you do, and he cannot bless your activities when you are deceitful, including how you handle your taxes."

We expect our employees to obey all of our instructions, not just the ones they decide to follow. How would you respond if an employee ignored your instructions or gave you a false report? Just as we will not let employees decide when they will tell us the truth and when they won't, we also must also always tell the truth.

Tom ran a small business employing 65 people. His accountant could clearly see that taxes were being avoided through false documentation. Instead of addressing the issue with Tom, the accountant began embezzling funds from the company, starting small, and working up until he finally got caught after $150,000 had disappeared. When confronted, he admitted stealing the money, but said to Tom, "Since you were cheating on your taxes, I just thought I would take some too." He also told Tom that if he were charged with a crime, he would turn in to the IRS a file of the false tax information. Intimidated, Tom allowed the thief to simply resign and walk away with the $150,000.

Although the IRS can only go back three years in correcting tax amounts based on a difference of opinion, failure to report income—any amount of income—is considered fraud, which has no statute of limitations. The tax collector can go back as far as possible to collect taxes, interest, and penalties—and you could end up in jail for tax evasion.

Issues of Opinion

Some tax issues are cloudy and not easily clarified. Having a legitimate difference of opinion over a tax situation is different from filing false returns. I have been clear with my accountant that I never want to be embarrassed during a tax review by any of the positions taken on my returns. John Wesley said, "Earn all you can, save all you can, and give all you can." I believe in saving on my taxes by using diligence and utilizing every deduction and element of the tax code that helps to save money and is honorable.

Failing to Pay Taxes

Some business owners get into trouble by filing tax returns but failing to pay the taxes as they're due, ultimately building up a large debt. Attorneys advertise about how they can help reduce your tax bill by tens of thousands of dollars. I view unpaid taxes as if they are another business debt—something that needs to be paid. King David writes, "The wicked borrow and do not repay" (Psalm 37:21, NIV).

Taxes are accrued on payroll, property, and profits as we go along, just like the outstanding invoices we owe to suppliers, bankers, credit card companies, and the landlord. I see no difference between a legitimate tax bill and other justifiable bills that we need to honor. If we owe taxes we cannot pay, we need to go to the appropriate government agency, confess our fault, explain our situation, and endeavor to work out a method of repayment.

Aiding and Abetting Others

Aside from keeping our own personal and business tax returns honest, we cannot assist others who may be engaged in underreporting taxes. Though we are not the tax police, we should not help others evade taxes. For example, we are required to furnish 1099 tax ID forms when paying individuals for work. Though cash-under-the-table payments are a common practice, we must operate our payroll with integrity. Moses writes, "Do not follow the crowd in doing wrong..." (Exodus 23:2, NIV). The only reason someone would want to be paid in cash, or with no 1099 issued, would be to underreport income.

Also, we need to check our motivation. Are we willing to pay cash under the table to help out a friend or someone in need? Or is our true motivation that we hope to receive a lower price? When we pay less with cash, we are receiving part of the "benefit" and have thus participated in sin. It's kind of like buying a stolen watch at a lower price.

While working with a Christian ministry, I hired a Christian contractor to paint a building for $4,000. The job was done over the summer, and he was paid by ministry check. In January, the bookkeeper realized we had failed to get the painter's tax ID number for sending out the 1099 form as required. When we asked for the tax number, he was outraged that he was going to receive a 1099. He said that he had already filed his taxes and didn't want to change the return. I suggested the only reason he didn't want a 1099 was that he was planning to underreport income. He hung up, but he ultimately received the dreaded 1099.

Burying Personal Expenses in a Business

Owners may be tempted to add personal items to the ledger as business expenses. In reality, this is another form of creating a false tax return. The tax code specifies how to divide business mileage and expenses from personal use. Looking for the most advantageous tax treatment is fine, but certifying a truck is used one hundred percent for business when it is not, is false.

Hobbies, personal travel, golf outings, and many other activities have been taken as tax deductions. When in doubt, allow an honest tax preparer to determine whether an item is a legitimate deduction or not.

Taking business property home is the same thing as burying expenses. One grocer fed his family by bringing food home every day. In reality, he was inadvertently avoiding income taxes on the value of the items he took home.

Use Taxes

Use taxes are commonly overlooked, often inadvertently. In most states that charge sales tax, a use tax is levied on businesses that purchase products from out-of-state vendors who are not required to collect sales tax from the state where the buyer is located. Check with your accountant, but generally these items, which may look like a better deal based on not paying sales tax, may not be such a good deal when you factor in the use tax.

Personal Liability

In some instances, business owners can be held personally liable for any shortfall in tax payments. Generally, with a corporation, any unpaid taxes are the responsibility of the corporation, not the individual. If the company goes bankrupt, the taxes go with the bankruptcy. However, depending on the circumstances, corporate officers may be held personally liable for the payment of payroll taxes. In addition, individuals have been and can be charged with fraud when filing tax documents that they knew to be false on behalf of a corporation.

When a business operates as a sole proprietorship, all tax liability, regardless of the source, falls to the individual owner. This includes the spouse when the owner is married.

Businesspeople in partnerships also need to be diligent. Any tax shortfall is a liability shared by each and every partner. If one or more partners do not, or cannot pay, the government will go after the partners with assets. In one instance, a construction partner failed to pay taxes by falsifying the books and pocketing the money. The IRS filed a tax judgment for $400,000 against both partners. Unfortunately, the honest partner was the only one with money, and he was forced to pay the $400,000, which wiped out his savings. Don't naively trust your partner. Make sure you know the situation in your partnership.

Ultimately, how we choose to come to grips with taxes is an integrity issue. Whether we underreport income, falsify expenses, bury personal items in the business' books, or help others avoid taxes, there is no middle ground. We are either people of integrity, or we are not. It's a choice we all have to make.

Case Study: To Claim or Not to Claim

Barbara and Christopher Crandon owned a Best Value printing company. Total revenue was $2.2 million per year, and reported taxable profits were $40,000 last year. All payroll taxes, included in the payroll records, were paid and up-to-date.

Each owner drove a car paid for one hundred percent by the company. Chris drove a covered pickup he used for customer deliveries, running errands, and picking up printing supplies as needed. Barbara did little business driving.

The Crandons had a part-time employee, Robert, who helped clean up every week. Robert was paid between $50 and $60 per week out of petty cash, with no employee record created. Also, Tina did bookkeeping a few hours a week and was paid in cash with no 1099 issued at year end.

Chris' mom, who was 84 years old and living on a very tight budget, was placed on the payroll at $1,000 a month, even though she did no work and never came to the office. Barbara often ordered personal items to be delivered to the print shop and charged those items on the business credit card. These items were expensed as general overhead.

When the building needed a roof replacement, due to leaking, at a cost of $15,000, the Crandons' accountant said he could try to take the entire $15,000 as an operating expense that year by claiming the work as a repair. He cautioned, however, that if the business were audited, the IRS could take the position that the work went beyond that of a repair and would need to be depreciated over time.

The business had a limited amount of walk-in traffic, and every year about $12,000 in cash payments were placed in Chris' pocket as "walking around money."

Question

If you were an IRS tax auditor, which transactions would you be interested in, and why?

CHAPTER 14

Hiring Illegal Workers

Depending on the estimate, twelve to eighteen million people currently live in the United States illegally. Many of these people are also *working* here illegally. What is the responsibility of business leaders regarding this issue?

Even though laws were broken when these illegal immigrants entered the U.S. or when they overstayed a visa, some people would argue that because they're here and a de facto part of our society, they should be granted some form of amnesty based on mercy. Others believe that our immigration laws should be enforced without exception. Deuteronomy 10:18 instructs us to feed and clothe the alien, and Moses tells us not to mistreat them (see Leviticus 19:33-34). Thus far, the United States has been very tolerant of those here illegally, and clearly, any immigration policy must be established in a spirit of justice, not vindictiveness. Treating anyone with disrespect is wrong.

The Requirement to Submit to the Rule of Law

Every nation must make laws; otherwise, everyone would do what is "right in his own eyes" (Judges 21:25). King Solomon writes, "Keep the king's commandment for the sake of your oath to God" (Ecclesiastes 8:2, NKJV), and "Whoever obeys his command will come to no harm" (Ecclesiastes 8:5, NIV). Peter instructs, "Submit yourselves for the Lord's sake to every human institution, whether to a king as the one in authority" (1 Peter 2:13). He concludes by saying, "For such is the will of God that by doing right you may silence the ignorance of foolish men" (1 Peter 2:15).

We must keep the law of the land, regardless of whether we agree or disagree with it. Let's face it, there will be some laws we dislike. However, when any law is flouted, ignored, or disobeyed, the whole system of law breaks down. As soon as one law is ignored, more violations of other laws will follow. If we allow one person or group of persons, no matter how large or compelling their argument, to decide which laws should be enforced and which should not, we undermine the rule of law on which our nation was founded. Thus, when business leaders take the position that it's okay to hire illegal workers, in violation of the law, they place themselves in opposition to one of the fundamental ideals of the American system. But it's not just a matter of patriotism; it's a matter of personal integrity. We have to decide whether or not we will be businesspeople of integrity.

The Rationale for Hiring Illegals

Peter owns a landscape business in California and knowingly employs workers who are in the U.S. illegally. Peter cites two reasons for his actions. First, he simply can't hire the needed workers on the open market. And if he did, their wages would be much higher, forcing him to raise prices and potentially lose customers.

When pressed, Peter acknowledges that he could hire legal residents, but cost is the big issue. "I just can't afford the higher wages," he says. Paul writes, "If anyone competes as an athlete, he does not win the prize unless he competes according to the rules" (2 Timothy 2:5). When we decide which rules to keep or break, and which laws to obey or disobey, where do we stop?

Deciding to break the law on hiring "because I need to in order to be competitive," is like a football lineman saying to the referee that holding on third down and ten, with the game on the line, should be disregarded because the lineman needs to protect the quarterback or the game will be lost. We would say that's absurd; you must compete within the rules.

Millions of illegal workers are employed by businesses under the guise that we need the workers and it keeps labor costs down. Many pundits speak of the economic reasons why we should look the other way, how this labor keeps the price of tomatoes down, or how people couldn't get landscaping done without this source of labor. However, when we start excusing sin and lawbreaking on the basis that the result is good, we have lost the moral battle.

From my own perspective, the labor costs are not as much of an issue as some people say. For example, in the mid-1960s, a guest farm worker program was stopped, resulting in a forty percent increase in farm worker wages. A forty percent increase in wages today would result in an increase of about ten dollars per year for fruit and vegetables, per household, according to Rich Lowry of *National Review* magazine. In addition, if wages were increasing and workers scarce, businesses would invest quickly in new and innovative technology, creating more and better jobs.

The "everybody's doing it" rationale is used by some, and disregard of the law is widespread. Moses writes, "Do not follow the crowd in doing wrong" (Exodus 23:2, NIV). In today's society, many people are running toward sin, pornography, illicit drug use, and fraud, but most of us see no reason to join the crowd. We know that God looks at each one of us and asks us to keep ourselves out of sin.

Hurting Yourself
King Solomon writes, "If you assist a thief, you only hurt yourself" (Proverbs 29:24, NLT). Ultimately, the unfettered

breaking of the law will break a society. Like sin, when we tolerate lawbreaking, we open up the floodgates for more.

First, when we violate the law, we set ourselves up to be charged with a crime. Even though most of the legislation targeting employers for hiring illegal aliens has been scantly enforced, when the political winds shift, such laws may be enforced with a vengeance and we don't want to get caught in the crossfire. The result could be fines, penalties, bad publicity, and possible jail time.

Looking the other way and ignoring wrongdoing establishes a benchmark that says breaking the law is okay, at least in some cases. As a consequence, others in your organization may take the liberty of breaking laws in other areas.

Hiring people who are in the country illegally makes reference-checking problematic at best. Criminal backgrounds are common. According to Jim Kouri, vice-president of the National Association of Chiefs of Police, illegal aliens comprise twenty-seven percent of the current U.S. inmate population. According to Heather McDonald of the Manhattan Institute, sixty percent of all outstanding arrest warrants in Los Angeles are for illegal residents. When we hire undocumented workers, we run a much higher risk of taking on an active criminal.

Keep in mind, a worker who is in the U.S. illegally has already broken one law, the law of legal entry. You may be getting more than you bargained for by hiring workers with possibly unsavory backgrounds.

Motivations That Encourage Hiring Illegal Residents

One motivation for hiring illegal workers is the opportunity to pay lower wages. In Arizona, and other southwestern border states, it's not uncommon to see people hanging around outside the local home improvement store, looking for someone to give them a temporary job. I have overheard several conversations among contractors who say, "Let's hire these illegals. We can get them much cheaper and they will work all day." By compromising their integrity, they not only break the law, but they also take advantage of the workers. Clearly, they are motivated by the opportunity for a "bargain," not by a willingness to pay wages competitive with the market.

Avoiding the payment and reporting of payroll taxes is another motivation for hiring illegal workers. One-third to one-half of illegal workers in the U.S. do not have Social Security and income taxes withheld. This is tax evasion, pure and simple, and the employer "saves" the part of the tax required to be paid to the government. I'm not a fan of high Social Security and income taxes, but we have a moral and legal responsibility to pay what is owed. The apostle Paul writes, "Render to all what is due them: tax to whom tax is due" (Romans 13:7). Wholesale evasion of payroll taxes creates a higher burden for the rest of society and makes additional tax evasion more likely.

Effect on American Society

Illegal immigration imposes a burden on the rest of society. The Center for Immigration Studies reports that the additional tax burden to taxpayers is $1,183 in California, $725 in Texas, and $700 in Arizona. Paul writes, "For each one will bear his own load" (Galatians 6:5). When we exploit the benefits of lower wages, tax evasion, and filling our employment ranks with undocumented workers, we are not bearing our own load. Part of our burden is shifted to others who do not receive the benefits we have received. It's like shoplifting. The thief gains the value of the stolen property if he doesn't get caught. But when the store has to raise its prices to compensate for the cost of stolen merchandise, every honest customer pays more. Employers who steal the benefits of hiring at lower wages and avoiding payroll taxes only push the social costs onto others.

Abuse of Workers

Hiring workers who are in the country illegally sets up possible workplace abuses. I realize that many employers of illegal workers do not engage in abusive employment tactics, but some do, placing the workers in a vulnerable position.

Some unscrupulous employers pay below the minimum wage, trusting that their illegal employees won't dare to complain. Overtime payment laws are often ignored, and workplace safety violations are more common. In extreme cases, employers fail to pay their employees at all. Moses writes, "Never take advantage of poor and destitute laborers, whether they are fellow Israelites or foreigners living in your towns. You must pay them their wages each day before sunset because they are poor and are counting on it. If you don't, they might cry out to the LORD against you, and it would be counted against you as sin" (Deuteronomy 24:14-15, NLT).

Employment laws are created to preserve a balance between employer's and worker's rights in the workplace. We may not agree with or like some workplace legislation, but we do not have the right to unilaterally ignore such regulations. Hiring illegal residents shifts the balance of power toward the employer.

Treating All Workers with Respect

All people, regardless of status, are entitled to be treated with kindness and respect. The Lord demands that we treat everybody well. Use of ethnic slurs, a demeaning tone of voice, or treating anybody with contempt is wrong. Some people who strongly oppose immigration—legal or illegal—use some pretty strong language.

Declining to offer a job to someone who is in the country illegally is not of itself a lack of respect, assuming we decline such employment respectfully. Hiring people according to the law, offering them fair and legal wages, and paying all required payroll taxes are all forms of granting respect, both to the worker and to society. Likewise, hiring illegally and paying below-market wages are signs of disrespect.

Another way to show people respect is to use the same hiring procedures for all workers. Substituting a higher or different standard for applicants who look and sound foreign violates the Biblical principle of not exercising partiality. We have many naturalized U.S. citizens and millions of foreign-born workers utilizing legitimate work visas. Our integrity dictates that we treat these people with complete respect.

Exercising Diligence

Employers need to accept responsibility for exercising reasonable diligence during the hiring process. King Solomon said, "Don't excuse yourself by saying, 'Look, we didn't know'" (Proverbs 24:12, NLT).

Many illegal workers use expertly forged documents, documents that would fool most of us. We may not catch every instance, but we must exercise due diligence. In general, you should be able to detect whether a worker's status is legal or illegal.

Case Study: Negligence Reaps Deadly Results

Wilbur owned and operated Green Valley Landscape Service in Arizona. Over the ten years he was in business, the company grew until it employed thirty people, including eight crew bosses.

Wilbur was unconcerned about the immigration status of his workers, asking only for a Social Security number for payment of payroll taxes. He suspected that several of the Social Security numbers provided were false, but he didn't make an issue of it. He asked for and received no personal documentation, and past employment references were not required. Wilbur's philosophy was that if he didn't like a worker, he would just fire him. No big deal.

Most workers were paid through the regular payroll system, with all taxes paid and withheld as required by law. At times, several workers would be hired for a day or two and paid with cash.

Wilbur's attitude toward his workers was reflected in the way he talked to them and about them. He often used rough language, tossing out ethnic slurs with little regard for others.

One afternoon, Wilbur stopped by to check on a crew and found them taking a break from the 108-degree heat. Using direct, demeaning statements, he told the crew leader to get up, and get going, and to stop being lazy. An argument ensued, and after quite a few words, Wilbur said, "You're all fired. Now, get out of here. I never want to see you back." Two of the crew members had not joined in the argument.

The crew boss stormed off, got into the company truck and raced away, along with the entire crew. Rather than returning to Green Valley's offices to pick up their own vehicles, the crew stopped by a local bar. Four hours later, they piled back in the truck to drive back to the landscape company. Two blocks from the bar, the crew boss ran a red light and struck a car, killing the other driver and one passenger in the truck. Four others were seriously injured.

Wilbur and Green Valley Landscaping were sued by the family of the killed driver and two of the landscaping workers. At the time of the accident, the crew boss was legally intoxicated, not a legal resident, and did not have a valid driver's license.

During the court proceedings, Wilbur admitted he had never checked the crew boss' background or legal employment status. As a result of publicity about the case, a payroll audit was conducted and Wilbur was fined for failing to report and pay some Social Security taxes. The courts also found Wilbur liable for negligence in the wrongful death and personal injury cases. The subsequent judgments forced him into personal and corporate bankruptcy.

Questions
- Identify the biblical principles that Wilbur violated.
- Did any one violation lead to his downfall?
- To what degree would you hold Wilbur responsible? Why?
- Who else shared responsibility?

CHAPTER 15

Sexual Harassment in the Workplace

S exual harassment is a reality in some workplaces. Multimillion dollar legal judgments have stung companies in the past. Though the law sets a standard, the Scriptures set a more important standard in keeping all workplaces free from sexual harassment.

In a 2006 study by *Glamour* magazine and Lawyers.com, thirty-five percent of women and seventeen percent of men said they had experienced sexual harassment at some time during their working career. Clearly, no person should have to endure any type of forced attention; be offered promotions in exchange for favors; or be subjected to crude or vulgar jokes, pictures, or any other offensive communication.

Harassment falls into two categories. The first is trading or promising jobs, promotions, or raises in return for attention or sexual contact. The second type of harassment is creating a poor environment that includes crude and explicit jokes, emails, and pictures. A workplace should be free of all harassment and disrespectful comments directed toward anyone at any time.

The most common complaint of sexual harassment is by woman claiming to be harassed by males. However, a trend is emerging of males who claim harassment by female managers, males by males, and females by females. Regardless of the type of harassment, it is wrong.

Quid Pro Quo

Simply put, any offer or inference of an offer to trade job advancement or a pay increase for sexual favors is wrong. Moses writes, "For the LORD your God is God of gods and Lord of lords, the great God, mighty and awesome, who shows no partiality and accepts no bribes" (Deuteronomy 10:17, NIV).

This Scripture gives us two key points. First, whenever we allow our personal feelings, desires, or self-indulgence to cloud or override our judgment, we have violated the biblical principle of showing no partiality.

These actions can take on several different forms. For example, Pat was involved with Barbara and offered her a job without going through the normal hiring and interviewing procedures. Six months after she started, the romance soured. Barbara repeatedly rebuffed Pat's further advances. Ultimately, Barbara sued, claiming she had been hired in return for her personal attention toward Pat. Simply put, there was a trade-off. Though Pat insisted the relationship was voluntary, he had placed himself in an untenable position by exercising very poor judgment. The romance could have, and should have, been kept out of the workplace.

A manager once told a staff member that she might get a departmental promotion if she would join him for dinner. She politely declined. Over the next three weeks, he asked her out on four occasions, and each time she declined the offer. When the new position was posted, she applied for the job but was not selected. She then sued for discrimination, contending that if she had dated the boss she would have landed the job. The boss testified that he had just been kidding and joking around, but the court held the company liable based on the boss' statements, joking or not, and his repeated attempts to ask out the female staff member.

In another case, a woman was asked out by her supervisor, who said with a wink, "If you want to keep your job, why not go to a movie with me." A complaint was filed, and the supervisor was reprimanded for what was perceived as a "go out with me or else" comment. New Jersey governor James McGreevy resigned in disgrace after allegations were made by a male friend that a job was provided in return for sexual favors.

Here's a simple guideline: Never—not even jokingly—suggest that an employee's job status or prospects for promotion have anything to do with his or her relationship with you. At all times, maintain a professional demeanor and distance with your employees and colleagues.

The Business Loses

Whenever a person is hired or promoted based on any measure other than merit, the business loses the best possible staff person, thus weakening the business.

Moreover, we lose our managing authority. King David writes, "Don't let those who trust in you be ashamed because of me" (Psalm 69:6, NLT). We need our staff members to trust and follow our leadership. People notice our involvement with others, and when they believe we are out of line or showing favoritism to anyone, especially those with whom we are involved, our credibility and authority are shattered.

Moses gave a stern warning, "For every breach of trust… he whom the judges condemn shall pay double to his neighbor" (Exodus 22:9). When we violate the trust placed in our hands, whether as a manager or a business owner, we create a breach of trust, and we will pay the price in the future.

A company manager was having an ongoing affair with a clerical staff person and recommended that person for a promotion into a supervisory position. Prior to the promotion being approved, the manager was questioned and cautioned about the qualifications of the person being promoted. Despite the expressed concerns, the promotion went through.

Later, senior management became aware that the new supervisor was performing poorly. Subsequently, they discovered the affair between the manager and the new supervisor. The senior vice president determined that the new supervisor needed to be demoted from the position and took that action. In addition, the manager who had made the appointment was dismissed on the basis that he had allowed his personal feelings and circumstances to cloud his judgment. The manager had breached the trust that had been place in his care, and thus he paid the penalty for that breech.

Managers have a responsibility to avoid even the appearance of improper actions. Some companies have established policies prohibiting the dating or involvement of people within the same company, department, or authority structure. Every business must establish appropriate policies governing employee interactions, and must maintain a zero tolerance policy for any "this for that" behavior.

A Hostile Environment

The second type of harassment is allowing a hostile environment to be created in the workplace. No one in the workplace should be subjected to inappropriate behavior, such as being grabbed or touched in any way without consent. Neither should anyone be subjected to off-color jokes, vulgar emails, explicit gestures, requests for sex, rumor and innuendo, offensive pictures, or vile comments. Management has a responsibility to ensure that the workplace is free of this type of behavior. One step is to establish a clear policy that such shenanigans will not be tolerated.

Emails and the forwarding of "humor" have resulted in large judgments against companies, causing more than one CEO to be discharged. King David writes, "I will refuse to look at anything vile and vulgar" (Psalm 101:3, NLT). We can and should be clear that the workplace is no place for this junk. Additionally, the use of Internet and email filters and a policy of prohibiting visits to "adult" Web sites can help to stem the flow of some of the garbage.

Revealing or suggestive pictures and explicit cartoons should be prohibited. Though the world abounds with pornography, we cannot allow it in the workplace. Courts have awarded large judgments in situations where management allowed "pinups" and other offensive material in the office.

Any comment referring to a person's anatomy is out of line. Complimenting someone's appearance is fine (as long as it doesn't become manipulative), but commenting on someone's "nice legs" definitely crosses the line. Overly personal comments can be made male to female, female to male, female to female or male to male. Same sex harassment cases are becoming increasingly common. Understandably, anyone can be uncomfortable when made the object of such observations and comments.

Physical contact is another type of harassment. Patting someone as he or she passes by, offering a hug or a kiss—even on the cheek—or placing a hand on the shoulder, arm, or hand may be viewed as unwanted contact.

Establishing a Policy

In today's business environment, companies need to establish clear policies prohibiting sexual harassment in order to maintain compliance with federal, state, and local laws. Seek legal assistance if you are unclear about complying with the laws.

Policies should be clearly posted, communicated, and enforced. Outline behavior that is not acceptable. In addition, establish a reporting system to allow a staff member to safely voice complaints. King Solomon writes, "Through presumption comes nothing but strife" (Proverbs 13:10, NASB). Clearly establishing the rules avoids presumption on anyone's part.

Investigating Concerns

Your policy should contain a procedure for how concerns will be raised and how those issues will be investigated. Legally and ethically, a company has a much greater responsibility for preventing harassment after an issue has been raised. Ignorance cannot be claimed.

Moses writes, "If it is told you and you have heard of it, then you shall inquire thoroughly" (Deuteronomy 17:4). We have a responsibility to act quickly and thoroughly when an issue is raised. Determine the facts: who did what, when, and to whom. Often, the information can be corroborated by another party or by other evidence. Paul writes, "The facts of every case must be established by the testimony of two or three witnesses" (2 Corinthians 13:1, NLT). In almost every case, when you act quickly, you can determine the correct facts.

Every complaint needs to be thoroughly examined from both sides, because as Solomon observes, "The first to present his case seems right, till another comes forward and questions him" (Proverbs 18:17, NIV). We always need to give both people an opportunity to respond and share their perspective.

Taking Action

King Solomon writes, "Righteousness exalts a nation" (Proverbs 14:34) and—I would add—a workplace. Harassment has no place on the job, but if it does occur, we must ensure that we have a righteous response.

Keep in mind that one incident of inappropriate behavior is enough to generate a complaint. Different people will have different sensitivities, tolerances, and personal standards. Martha went to her company's human resources manager, complaining about being copied into broadcast emails containing off-color humor. The HR manager wisely contacted the offending person to reinforce the company's policy of not allowing such material in the workplace and firmly instructed the practice to stop.

If we allow one incident to go by without some type of discipline, it's like saying that a little sin is okay. But a little sin is *not* okay; a little harassment is *not* okay. In most cases, a quick and stern rebuke will stop the practice.

In another instance, a female complained that her boss occasionally touched her arm. Though the intent was innocent in this case, her sensitivity needed to be honored. The manager was asked to refrain from touching her.

Other cases may require more intervention, such as when a manager or supervisor allegedly abuses power by asking for favors. Some cases are difficult to determine, turning into a "he said, she said" situation. Generally, however, a pattern of behavior will emerge that will confirm the allegations.

Justice must be the framework for any outcome. I have seen cases where male supervisors go merrily along while their female staff members feel they need to leave their jobs. I know of another case where a male manager harassed several male workers, who left the company rather than continue to put up with the aggravation. Some managers may not take action, looking at incidents as "boys will be boys," but this perspective fails to correct the problem. If you ask a staff member to stop telling off-color jokes, and then laugh about it, you haven't really taken any action. Other times, we may not want to confront a star performer, but if we fail to take action, we violate the principle of not showing partiality and deprive someone of justice.

Be familiar with current regulations requiring the investigation and discipline of harassment complaints, and make sure your business complies. Consult an attorney when in doubt.

No Retaliation

Part of any harassment policy must be a commitment never to allow retribution after a complaint has been made, regardless of the feelings involved. We have a responsibility to treat both parties with respect and dignity after a complaint has been made.

When Fred attempted to kiss Francis at the office, she rebuffed the attempt and subsequently reported the incident in accordance with the HR harassment policy procedure. At

Fred's next performance review, he was graded significantly lower than previous reviews, raising the legitimate issue that the lower review was based on the complaint filed, not on a decrease in work performance.

Set a High Personal Standard

The first step in avoiding harassment is setting and maintaining your own high standard. Avoiding any appearance of wrongdoing is a good first step. I realize that in today's business environment men and woman are thrust together much more than in past generations. However, avoiding any appearance of impropriety is key. When having a private conversation with someone of the opposite sex, try to keep the office door open, even an inch. Also, avoid as much as possible traveling, meeting, or eating meals in circumstances that might be viewed as compromising.

When someone asks me, "Do you want to hear a good joke?" I often respond, "Would you tell the joke to a minister?" If the answer is no, then I don't need to hear that joke. When we hear or see anything inappropriate, we need to take action. We don't need to take it as a sermon opportunity; we simply need to explain that the behavior is not acceptable and make sure that any offensive behavior is eliminated.

A leader's personal standard of behavior will set the tone for the company. We cannot tolerate sin in the camp. Joshua 7:10-26 tells the story of how the people of Israel suffered defeat because of the sin of one family. Likewise, our businesses will suffer if we allow sin—any sin—to continue under our watch.

Case Study: Misbehavior in Need of Repair

Tom was the owner of a Daisy Auto dealership. In the repair shop, several pictures of scantily clad women were posted. Sally, the billing clerk, had complained to Tom several times that when she went into the garage to check billing questions she was repeatedly asked if she wanted to "get into the back seat for a while." The department manager told his technicians to cut out the chatter, because Sally had complained, and she "apparently didn't want to have a good time."

Albert, one of the sales managers, had expressed an interest in spending time with Ted, promising better floor time if he would "cooperate." When Ted refused, he was given poor assignments. He complained to Tom, who just laughed, and brushed off the complaint.

Wilma was asked out several times by her manager, Porter, who said, "I can help you get ahead if you let me help you." After several weeks of nonstop advances, she complained to Tom, who sternly warned Porter to cease and desist immediately, and to continue to give her floor time on the same basis as the other salespeople.

Questions
- What steps could the service manager have taken to be more effective?
- Should Tom have been aware of the posted pictures?
- Did Tom treat both harassment claims equally?
- In your opinion, was the dealership open to a harassment claim by Sally? Why or why not?
- Do you believe Ted had a valid claim for management failing to take action? Why or why not?
- Did Wilma have a valid complaint for management's failure to take action? Why or why not?

CHAPTER 16

The Real Bottom Line

In these chapters, we have covered many of the challenges we face in being faithful men and women in business. Ultimately, we each will decide whether or not to be a person of integrity. Scripture provides an outstanding word picture of God's commitment to people of integrity: "For the eyes of the Lord move to and fro throughout the earth that He may strongly support those whose heart is completely His" (2 Chronicles 16:9). Imagine, when you have committed your heart totally to the Lord, He will literally be looking for ways to strongly support you!

How many businesspeople have said, "I want to be a person of integrity, but I lack the power to do so"? Christian financial advisor Larry Burkett gave an example of a fellow who was being baptized. As he was being immersed, he held his wallet above the water, symbolizing his willingness to give everything to God except his wallet. Likewise, some business leaders struggle with giving everything to the Lord and becoming people of complete integrity.

We are unable to live lives of integrity in our own strength. The only way we can truly succeed is through the indwelling empowerment of the Holy Sprit. That's why the apostle Paul encourages us to "be filled with the Spirit" (Ephesians 5:18, NIV).

Jesus himself was tempted, so we need to understand that temptation will follow us. The key is in how we choose to work through those temptations.

Ron's Struggle

A contractor named Ron chose the name Fish Construction for his business as a symbol that he was a Christian and his business was a Christian business. He attended church regularly, advertised in the Christian directory and on Christian radio, and the fish symbol was prominently displayed on his work trucks, business cards, and letterhead.

At times, Ron scheduled more work than his company could complete because he wanted to avoid downtime between jobs. When he got behind, he started some jobs later than agreed and finished other jobs late. He rationalized that by staying busy and overlapping projects, he was being a good steward of his time.

When cash flow was slow, Ron delayed payments to his suppliers. He could have borrowed on a line of credit, but borrowing would have increased his expenses, so making his suppliers wait a little longer seemed like better business.

At times, Ron discovered he had underbid on a job and was in danger of losing money. To avoid taking a loss, several times he substituted lesser quality materials than called for in the construction specifications. He thought, *Why should I lose money on a job when the lesser quality materials would still meet the need?*

Over the years, Ron prospered financially, and many people admired him for his successes. Inside, however, Ron was battling with his conscience. He knew that cutting corners was not quite right, but it seemed that God was blessing his business, so why should he worry? His customers became frustrated and angry when work was completed late, and some days Ron was so anxious he would not answer his cell phone. Some nights, he was restless and unable to sleep.

Though Ron had accepted Jesus as Lord and Savior of his life, he was struggling with the issue of placing the Lord in charge of every aspect of his life. In our human nature, we tend to crown ourselves king. Paul writes, "The man without the Spirit does not accept the things that come from the Sprit of God, for they are foolishnesses to him, and he cannot understand them, because they are spiritually discerned" (1 Corinthians 2:14, NIV). Until we commit ourselves fully to Jesus Christ as our Lord and Savior in every aspect of our lives, we have placed ourselves on the throne.

Every Person's Battle

Paul chastised the Corinthians for being worldly (1 Corinthians 3:1-3), and wrote in his letter to the Romans, "Those who live according to the sinful nature have their minds set on what nature desires; but those who live in accordance with the Spirit have their minds set on what the Spirit desires" (Romans 8:5, NIV). In business, as in all of life, we will have a constant battle between placing ourselves on the throne or giving the Lord complete control. Placing ourselves in charge creates inner conflict. Until we decide to fully surrender our will to God's will, our spiritual lives and our business lives will go up and down.

Luke, in his Gospel, writes that the Lord wants "to rescue us from the hand of our enemies and to enable us to serve him without fear in holiness and righteousness before him all our days" (Luke 1:74-75, NIV). We, then, make the choice to place God, and God alone, on the throne by calling on Him to give us the power to do what we cannot do in our own strength. Until we make this choice, we cannot do what we ought to do, and we will do what we ought not to do. There will always be a war raging between our human will and the divine will unless we fully surrender to Jesus—not merely as Savior through His free gift of salvation, but also by then following Him in all ways as Lord. It is selfish to accept God's gift of love and redemption without honoring Him by surrendering to His ways each moment of every day.

The great truth is that we alone make the choice to place God on the throne of our lives, and we alone call on the Holy Sprit for the strength required to lead holy, pure, and empowered lives. Sadly, many who profess to be Christians have not learned to make this choice—or they simply haven't made it.

If you have not taken the step of making Jesus Lord over every area of your life, including your business, you may do so right now. The hallmark of a true Christian in business is taking this step of spiritual maturity—this is true integrity.

First, *admit your need.* Confess to the Lord that you have held something back, not done what He has asked of you, or disobeyed His teaching. Tell Him you want to hand everything over now as your love gift to Him.

Second, *ask God to cleanse you* of all unrighteousness and dedicate yourself totally to the Lord. As Paul writes, "I urge you therefore, brethren, by the mercies of God, to present your bodies a living and holy sacrifice, acceptable to God, which is your spiritual service of worship" (Romans 12:1).

Third, *believe God's promises,* by faith, that He will do a work in your life and grant an empowerment you do not have in your own strength, "that we might receive the promise of the Sprit through faith" (Galatians 3:14).

Use Scripture for Your Decisions

In order to sustain your holy walk with God, make daily Bible reading a part of your schedule. Put it on your calendar. Daily Bible reading is an important way to seek, learn, and apply God's direction in your business. When looking at Scripture, ask several questions:

1. Is there a command to obey? For example, the Ten Commandments are clearly orders to obey. Other times, we apply principles found in Scripture, such as when David writes, "The wicked borrows and does not pay back" (Psalm 37:21),

which demonstrates that paying back loans is a command for obedience. When Scripture gives us these directives, we simply need to comply.

2. Does the Scripture give us a warning or guideline to heed? The prophet Habakkuk writes, "Will not your creditors rise up suddenly?" (Habakkuk 2:7), and Solomon writes, "The borrower becomes the lender's slave" (Proverbs 22:7). These passages do not prohibit borrowing, but they do offer a cautionary guideline. When you read the fine print in a loan agreement, you become aware that you have given the lender a lot of control over your life, especially if you can't pay.

3. What is the Biblical model? Matthew 18:15-17 provides a model to follow when we believe we have been offended. We are first to go to the other person alone to seek resolution. If that doesn't work, we're to go back with another person along to mediate. Finally, we're to bring the matter to the church, if necessary. When someone offends us, we have a Biblical model we can employ. Likewise, many passages provide blueprints for other circumstances.

4. Is there a promise or assurance we should claim? Malachi writes, "'Bring the whole tithe into the storehouse, so that there may be food in my house, and test Me now in this,' says the Lord of hosts, 'if I will not open for you the windows of heaven and pour out for you a blessing until it overflows'" (Malachi 3:10). In this instance, when we are obedient and tithe, the Lord's promise is to meet our needs.

5. What is the lesson? Paul writes, "All Scripture is inspired by God and profitable for teaching, for reproof, for correction, for training in righteousness" (2 Timothy 3:16). For example, I have at times not been the best communicator, not using enough detail to be clear. Reading Solomon's words, "Through presumption comes nothing but strife" (Proverbs 13:10), convicted me that I needed to become more clear and concise in my communication.

6. What in our lives requires correction? For example, if we tend to complain, even to ourselves, we need to change our

attitude and submit to Scripture: "Do all things without grumbling or disputing" (Philippians 2:14).

Daily Prayer

Because we spend a lot of time at work, we need to include work issues in our prayer lives. Paul writes, "Pray without ceasing" (1 Thessalonians 5:17), so clearly we must continue to pray about work issues.

For example, if we are in conflict with a coworker, we should ask God to give us the wisdom and insight to peaceably resolve the issue. We should ask God to show us the customers who will truly benefit from our product or service. When we pray about our daily schedules, we should ask God to make us good stewards of our time and give us insight into our business issues.

The Consecrated Business Leader

In 1 Corinthians 3:1-3, Paul gives us a word picture that applies to every Christian: "Brothers, I could not address you as spiritual but as worldly—mere infants in Christ. I gave you milk, not solid food, for you were not yet ready for it. Indeed, you are still not ready. You are still worldly" (NIV). Every day, perhaps every hour, we will be tempted to short-circuit our commitment to God's principles in our businesses, whether it's ignoring a customer concern, treating a vendor harshly, or not being completely honest with a colleague.

The writer of Hebrews instructs us to move further in our faith: "Therefore let us leave the elementary teachings about Christ and go on to maturity, not laying again the foundation of repentance from acts that lead to death" (Hebrews 6:1, NIV). As business leaders we need to decide whether we are going to totally consecrate ourselves and our businesses to the Lord. Are we willing to be totally sold out to be His disciples, wherever we are, whatever we are doing, regardless of our circumstances?

God's Provision

Scripture tells us to call upon the Lord and claim His promises. Luke writes, "We are witnesses of these things, and so is the Holy Spirit, whom God has given to those who obey him" (Acts 5:32, NIV). The apostle John writes, "But if we walk in the light, as he is in the light, we have fellowship with one another, and the blood of Jesus, his Son, purifies us from all sin" (1 John 1:7, NIV). When Jesus commissioned Paul to serve him, he sent him "to open their eyes and turn them from darkness to light, and from the power of Satan to God" (Acts 26:18, NIV).

We have the opportunity to call upon the Lord to fill us with His Holy Sprit and give us the strength to follow Him completely and obediently. Paul writes, "May God himself, the God of peace, sanctify you through and through. May your whole sprit, soul and body be kept blameless at the coming of our Lord Jesus Christ. The one who calls you is faithful and he will do it" (1 Thessalonians 5:23-24, NIV).

As we make a personal decision to lay everything at God's feet, to place everything on His altar, and place ourselves totally under His control, the Lord will give us the strength and wisdom to lead holy, godly lives in whatever circumstances we find ourselves. Paul tells us to put on the full armor of God (see Ephesians 6:10-18). A warrior going into battle needs every resource at his disposal. Some items, such as a rifle, are for offensive purposes; others, such as flak jackets and helmets, are for defending ourselves. No combatant would voluntarily go into battle without being fully prepared, and we should do no less. Only by putting on the full armor of God every day and calling on the Lord to give us the empowerment of the Holy Sprit can we navigate the minefield of the business world.

Our Choice

Given God's offer to fill us with the Holy Spirit and the promises of Scripture that we can claim, we still have to decide whether or not we will enthusiastically embrace and claim those promises. The choice we make will influence everything in our lives and businesses. We might be tempted to say, "I will change after I get the next promotion, win that large customer, or turn the corner and become profitable." However, we need to make that decision *today,* before we face the consequences of our disobedience, no matter what situation we are in. With God's Word and His Holy Spirit filling our thoughts and actions, we can march out in faith with God's empowerment and truly make a difference in the world for Christ.

John Wesley, the famed eighteenth-century preacher and writer, would not allow personal testimonies of God's grace and power that were more than one week old. He believed that every Christian should have fresh, new stories. How real is the Lord in our lives? How has Christ changed us in what we do and how we do it? When we walk obediently with Him who saves us, we create new stories of how the Lord has worked in our lives.

Peter's Battle

Five years ago, Peter started River Marketing, an advertising company employing twelve people. The company was struggling because as business grew, Peter kept adding more staff. So instead of increasing profits, he started losing money.

Peter was very creative, great at developing customer relationships, but weak on financial controls and managing staff. He believed that the answer to his challenges was to work more hours. He asked his small staff to work harder, believing that was the key issue.

As a result of his time commitment at work, his marriage was strained. His staff turnover was high, due to the increased pressure, and the balance sheet was sinking further into the red. The more he tried and the harder he worked, the further behind he fell. He began quoting every job himself, at times overpromising just to get the business needed to stay afloat. However, he lost several key customers due to failed promises with work delivery.

Peter came to the place where he realized he was trying to do everything in his own strength. He took a weekend alone with the Lord for prayer and reflection, and to seek a new direction for his life. He came to understand that while he had accepted Jesus as Lord and Savior, he had not placed Him on the throne of his life. Peter's life was evidence of the struggle between himself and the Lord for full control. That weekend, Peter asked the Lord to take full control in every aspect of his life. He made the decision to surrender everything to Christ, including his business.

After the weekend retreat, Peter was a changed man, and it was a change that lasted for his lifetime. The following Monday, a customer called offering a large contract if the work could be completed within two weeks. Peter was tempted, but he knew that accepting the work would cause him to dishonor other promises. Ultimately, he declined the job, much to the appreciation of the customer, who respected his honesty.

Every day, Peter took time—time he used to think he didn't have—to read Scripture and pray. As he committed this time to the Lord, his schedule flowed much more smoothly, projects came together better, and the business stabilized.

A few months later, Peter was approached by a larger advertising agency about merging operations. At first, he was reluctant to consider the offer; after all, he liked being his own boss. As he prayed for guidance, however, he came to see that if he accepted the merger, he would be able to focus all his time and energy with customers and creativity, and not be distracted with accounting and management, tasks he wasn't very good at.

He placed his business on God's altar with the prayer "Your will be done." As a result he received the peace to go ahead with the merger. The cash he received allowed him to pay off all his creditors and put some money aside for future retirement. He was able to maintain a healthy balance between work and family, resulting in a much stronger marriage and family relationship. Not only that, but now he had a testimony, a lifetime story to tell for the Lord.

The Real Bottom Line

Earlier in my career, I was CEO and president of the fourth-largest import/export company in the United States. By the world's standards, this was a coveted business position. The power and prestige of my job allowed me to shake hands with U.S. Presidents and attend exclusive gatherings with other business, political, and cultural leaders. Frequently, I was sought after for my skills. And yet I never achieved the satisfaction and success I longed for until I turned my life completely over to the Lord, accepting His gift of salvation, and then His indwelling Spirit each day. Many times, my faith was tested. In our fast-paced, bottom-line-driven world, I was often tempted to go my own way, rather than walk on God's path. Yet God was the one who kept my bottom line where it needed to be.

As you go forward in your business life, what really matters is not your position, power, or financial reward. What really matters is being obedient to the Lord in everything you do. Jesus said, "Seek first His kingdom and His righteousness, and all these things will be added to you. So do not worry about tomorrow; for tomorrow will care for itself. Each day has enough trouble of its own" (Matthew 6:33-34). Your treasures are in heaven in those who will be there as a result of your godly business life.

Paul writes, "The peace of God, which surpasses all comprehension, will guard your hearts and your minds in Christ Jesus" (Philippians 4:7). You, and all followers of Christ, can experience that peace as the storms of business rage around us—and that is the real bottom line.

Do you have a right relationship with God?

W ithout a right relationship with God our lives are very distant from Him, so distant that we do not even know who He is. This great distance causes us to go our own way, which causes further distance from what He intended for our lives. This spiritual separation causes us to constantly feel unsettled physically, emotionally, and intellectually. You may never have realized this connection before. Enjoying a rich relationship with God is the foundation for every other area of our lives, including our family, friends, and business.

An understanding and acceptance that God loves us and wants to be close to us is the beginning of all wisdom and true contentment (John 3:16). Jesus died for our willful disobedience going through life our own way. You know you have fallen short, right?

His free gift of peace, purpose and abundant life eludes us until we recognize that we are each separated from Him and His ways through our disobedience, which is called sin. Yet Jesus paid the price for our sinful nature while we were in a sinful attitude of mind and deed (Proverbs 14:12, Romans 6:23).

God provided a way for us to close the gap between Himself and mankind with the death of Jesus on the cross. Jesus paid the penalty for our sinfulness and showed us how to live a life in right relationship to Him (I Peter 3:18).

The choice is ours. Each of us knows if we have a right relationship with God or not. But we may not all know how to have this for our own lives. God has given us a free choice – follow Him for an abundant life of forgiveness, peace, purpose and fulfillment eternally, or to continue on our own way which brings destruction to ourselves and others. If we are genuinely sorry for disobeying God, are willing to turn from our own ways to follow Him, and then daily, moment-by-moment, allow Him to direct our lives as Lord and Savior, we will have a right relationship with Him for all eternity (Romans 10:9, Revelation 3:20).

These are the steps to a right relationship with God:

1. Admit your need of God and tell Him you are sorry for your sinfulness.

2. Be willing to turn from your sinfulness and turn toward Him (I John 1:9).

3. Believe by faith that Jesus, God's Son, died on the cross, rose from the grave, and now offers you forgiveness of sin (Ephesians 2:8-9).

4. Invite Jesus Christ to come into your life and to take control of your life through the Holy Spirit (Revelation 3:20).

Someone is waiting right now to answer your questions, pray with you, and help you to know how to lead a life pleasing in right relationship to God through Jesus Christ. You do not need to wonder, or continue thinking that if you are a good person God will forgive you and offer eternal life. You can know for certain. If you have never understood this before, or have unanswered questions, I pray you will call **1-888-NeedHim**. Only God knows the span of our life, tomorrow may be too late. Do not put it off another minute. Enjoy a new life with Christ!

About the Author

Steve Marr has learned from 36 years of business experience that God's way works. As an author, speaker and business consultant, Marr helps companies and organizations apply the ancient wisdom of the Bible to avoid the common mistakes and headaches of growing a business.

Marr's experience comes from serving as the CEO of the fourth largest import-export firm in the United States. Now he pairs that practical experience with the wisdom of the Bible. Marr uses spiritual and practical insight to pinpoint issues and recommend actions that bring lasting personal and business success.

Through one-on-one consulting, Marr connects with business leaders and helps them apply the Bible's wisdom. He offers practical advice and solutions that help business owners get started, move to the next level, or respond to a crisis that threatens their company.

Marr has written several books including the workplace devotional guide *Business Proverbs*, *Roadmap to Success* and *Blueprint for Integrity*. Marr also shares his written insights through a syndicated monthly business column that appears in over 30 outlets across the U.S.

Since 1998 Marr has offered advice through the one-minute radio spot "Business Proverbs," which can be heard on over 1,000 radio stations internationally. Marr also speaks at conferences and offers seminars for businesses and organizations. He's worked with the Billy Graham Center for Evangelism, the Salvation Army, appeared on *The 700 Club* and consulted for Family Life Radio.

Applying the ancient wisdom of the Bible to today's business situations is the heart and soul of Marr's work. He lives in Anthem, Arizona, with his family.

Ask Steve. He can help you find peace of mind, hope and satisfaction in doing business God's way. Visit his web site at BusinessProverbs.com to find out more.

CROWN FINANCIAL MINISTRIES

True Financial Freedom

OUR VISION

Crown Financial Ministries' vision is to see followers of Christ in every nation faithfully living by God's financial principles in every area of their lives.

OUR MISSION

Our primary mission is to equip people worldwide to learn, apply, and teach God's financial principles so they may know Christ more intimately, be free to serve Him, and help fund the Great Commission.

OUR CORE VALUES

Crown strives to be a Christ-centered, Bible-based ministry whose core values include recognition of God's ownership of all things, the need to pray about everything, and the desire to equip and serve others with excellence while teaching in ways understood by all cultures and generations.

OUR MAJOR OBJECTIVE

Our major objective is to teach God's financial principles to 300 million people by September 15, 2015.

———◆———

As an interdenominational Christian ministry, Crown is the largest ministry in the world dedicated to equipping church and marketplace leaders to know, apply, and teach people how to handle money God's way. With the help of generous donors around the globe, today Crown reaches millions each year through radio, Internet, publishing, seminars, small group studies, catalytic events, and a globally dispersed team of staff and volunteers.

To learn more about Crown Financial Ministries or to obtain materials that help teach God's financial principles in your church or community, visit us online at Crown.org or call 1-800-722-1976.

More Great
Business Books
from

Bridge-Logos

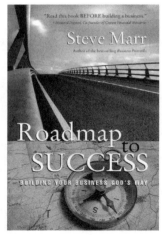

Also by
Steve Marr

Roadmap to Success: Building
Your Business God's Way
A complete, step-by-step guide
to starting a new business or
growing an existing one.

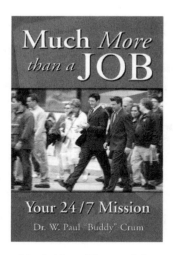

Much More Than a Job:
Your 24/7 Mission
Discover your mission in the
marketplace through vision,
planning, stewardship, ethics
and hearing God in your
work arena.

24 Keys to Complete Success
Shape your attitude, define
your goals, set priorities and use
your God-given talents to
succeed in business—and in life.

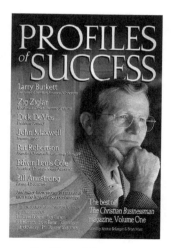

Profiles of Success
Inspiring accounts of successful
Christians in business and how they
got where they are.

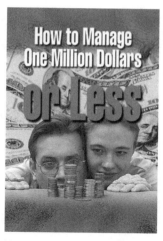

**How to Manage a Million
Dollars or Less**
29 top financial experts give advice
on financial management for your
business and personal life.

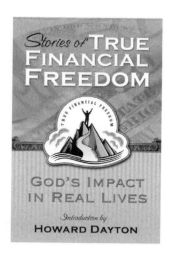

**Stories of True
Financial Freedom**
God's impact in the real lives of
people who were able to turn
financial disaster into victory.
(From Crown Financial
Ministries)

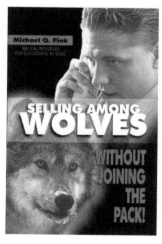

**Selling Among Wolves
Without Joining the Pack**
Proven strategies to make
great sales, based on biblical
principles. Field tested in
competitive selling
environments with
astounding success.